LIVING DESIGN

JAMIE DURIE & NADINE BUSH

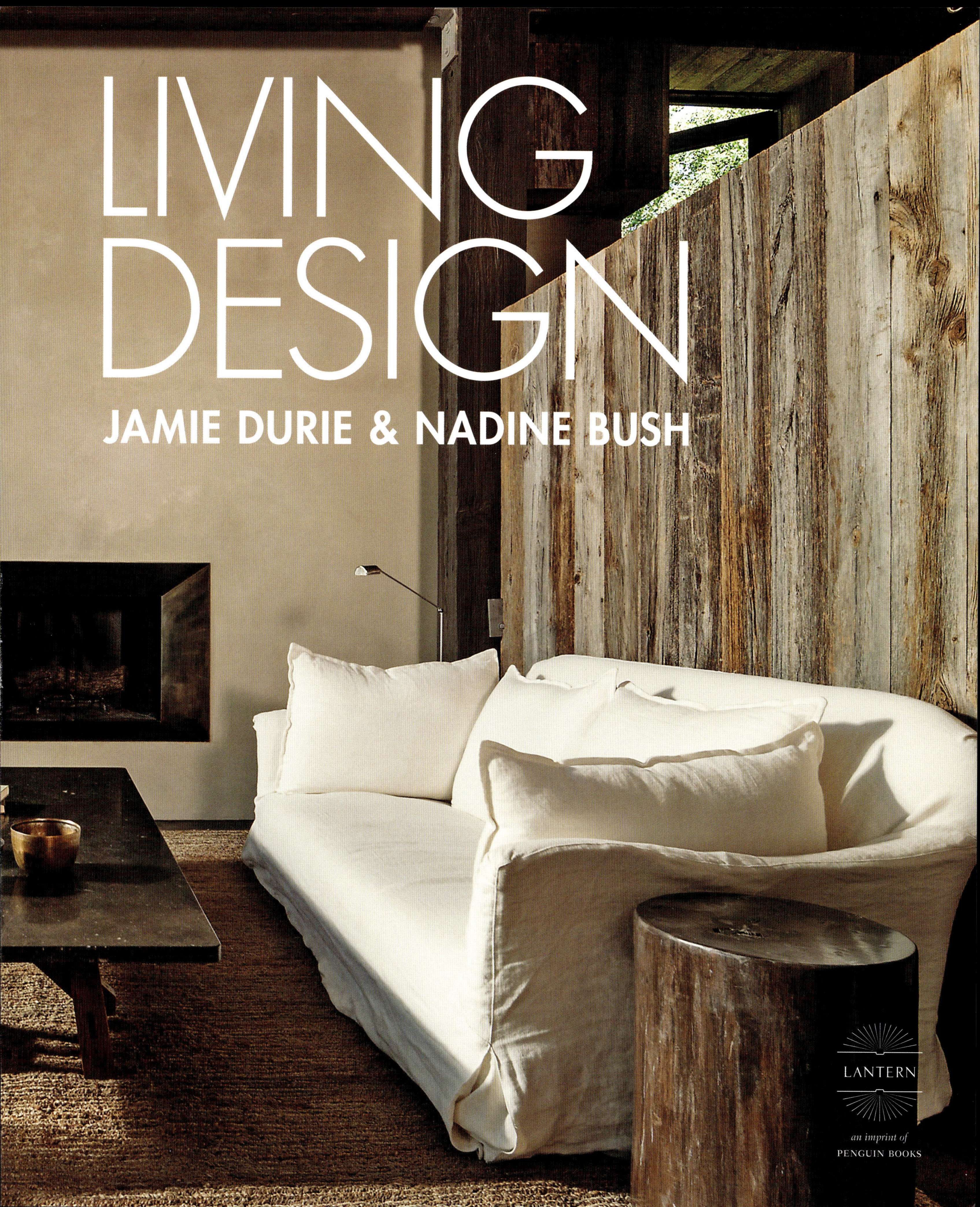

LANTERN

an imprint of
PENGUIN BOOKS

It's only natural 1

INTERIORS 5

OUR TRANSTERIOR DESIGN PHILOSOPHY 63

INSPIRATION IS EVERYWHERE 95

BRINGING THE OUTDOORS IN 147

TEN ROOMS 187

TRANSTERIOR LIVING 235

About Jamie & Nadine 307
Acknowledgements 308
Stockist list 310
Photography & design credits 312
Index 313

IT'S ONLY NATURAL

I am going to talk a lot in this book about nature as an inspiration for my furniture and interior design. Why are so many of us so obsessed with nature? In a nutshell, I think it's because we are all a part of nature, and we are slowly gaining a deeper spiritual and intellectual understanding of this. It is starting to dawn on us that we no longer have the perfect environment we once had. We are returning to nature in so many ways, feeling the need to draw her closer to us.

In an almost subliminal response, we are starting to arrange our post-industrial surroundings so that they are abundant with natural elements, living and non-living.

Did somebody tell us to start using more naturally inspired shapes, textures, proportions, colours and prints in our lives or did we all just wake up to it one day? There is a movement, let's call it a 'Natural Revolution'. We are strapped in for the ideological ride of our lives, full of organic stimulation. Mother Nature is making her point, and not a moment too soon.

We realise we have been living in an unsustainable way, disconnected from nature, and obsessed with technology. I believe the trend of wanting more just for the sake of it is finally starting to give way. Hard-working city slickers are turning to the great outdoors in search of inner peace, balance and restoration. Reconnecting with nature is like plugging yourself into an organic charger.

You can forge a deep connection with nature in many ways. We can't always take a walk through a forest of 1100-year-old Californian redwoods (something I was lucky enough to do recently). What we can do is try to bridge the gap between indoors and outdoors, something I've devoted the past two decades to in my work as a landscape designer. Ten years ago, I found another way to bring people closer to nature by moving from landscape design to interior and furniture design. Today, more of my clients sit on my furniture than walk through my gardens.

Interestingly, I've never felt more fulfilled, in terms of work, than I do now because I get to touch many more people with the design of a single chair that I've lovingly engineered into what the team and I believe to be the perfect ergonomic form than I ever did with landscape design. Through furniture design I get to share carefully considered proportions with the end user always in mind. I use natural materials and finishes that make the owner of the piece feel they now have a functional representation of nature itself, intimately connected to themselves in ways they might not have even realised they needed.

The textile industry has always been a leader in mimicking nature in prints and textures. I can get lost for days wandering through the many floors of the New York Design Depot, an amazing one-stop central supply hub where international designers can buy furniture, fabrics and wallpapers and other interior decorations for their clients.

We can connect 'naturally' not just by spending time in a natural environment, but also by bringing nature into our homes. Our world is evolving into a new place without doors or barriers, and no specific boundaries between indoors and outdoors.

One further step in this journey is to draw from nature's palette and blend it into the home. This is how Nadine and I originated our 'transterior' philosophy, which we discuss later. From the colours we choose to the floors we walk on, from the lights that illuminate to the tiles that decorate, every element in our home, every material, every shape, texture and choice we make can derive from nature.

So, let's begin this journey together, as we explore and discover old and new ways of reintroducing nature into our homes with the same amount of gusto that we took our homes out into nature.

Our Brickwood coffee table and Bolo lamp mix the raw and refined.

KATE MOSS

INTERIORS

OUR DESIGN DNA

All designers have their own 'design DNA'. Basically, ours is all about a deep connection with and respect for nature, through the subtle blending of natural and man-made materials and spatial connection. Nature is our 'design driver', a never-ending source of inspiration. Another distinctive feature of our design style is that we strive for innovation through the use of unique design and engineering and sustainable practices and products.

Our design DNA plays out in three simple ways:

1. The built form in architecture, furniture, interior or landscape takes on shapes, textures or colours that exist in nature.
2. The built form is integrated into the site or space that surrounds it.
3. There is an open connection and integration between nature and the built form.

Over the years I have noticed that there is a common thread in the work of the designers I love – they all use nature as a primary source of inspiration. I really like, for instance, Marc Newson's multiple applications of the honeycomb pattern, from the texture on the Qantas business class seats to the carpets he has designed, and one of his greatest pieces, the solid white carrara marble honeycomb wall unit. I also greatly admire Antoni Gaudí's incredible tree-like columns in the interior of the yet-to-be-completed La Sagrada Família basilica in Barcelona.

The ceiling, supported by tree-like columns, in the Gaudí basilica.

It is easy to see why so many designers have been inspired by nature over the years. Every leaf margin, vein direction, branch configuration and flower petal is unique, so there is an infinite supply of design concepts to draw from. We are all intrinsically connected to nature, and I like to draw upon that connection whatever I am designing – outdoor rooms, interiors and even furniture. The aim is to make people feel they are getting a bit closer to Mother Nature herself, whether they are indoors or outdoors.

Here's how it works. The architecture of the branches of a tree might inspire the structural integrity of a chair or dining table. The colour of naturally oiled maple or walnut timber might provide those deep, dark hues that lend a piece of furniture its sense of quality or a room a sense of establishment and depth. The tactile feeling of leather might be what draws you to sit on a chair made of leather and wood. It is the organic combination of the two that makes the chair so pleasant. The leather is like the smooth bark on the tree, if you like.

Ever since I was little, working with wood has been one of my greatest joys. I remember, at the age of eight, sitting on the steps of my mother's house carving a sailfish from cedar. When I was twelve, my grandfather made me a lathe out of an old washing machine motor, which I used to make wine goblets from scraps of maranti wood. Timber can be shaped into so many different forms, because of its strength, character and stability. We trust the durability of wood and its natural form and texture, and so we trust the feeling we get when we walk into a room lined with woodgrain panels.

What I love about nature is that it not only brings us geometrics like honeycomb or the perfect parallel lines in the veins of bamboo, but it also teaches us about freeform shapes and even proportion. To me, it really is the greatest mentor.

John Lautner's iconic Elrod House in Palm Springs, has interiors by Arthur Elrod. The Jetsons' style aesthetic allows the natural light and the surrounds to become a part of the home through its concrete spider-like domed roof.

OUR INTERIOR DESIGN STYLE

'Natural modern interiors' or 'raw luxury' is how I would describe our signature interior design style. I value recycling, repurposing, anything handmade, and I am a passionate hunter and gatherer. My many travels to exotic locations around the globe act as my secondary 'design driver'.

There is also a slight eclecticism to our interior style, which is influenced by mid-century modern architecture. This movement is named for the post-war period from 1945 to 1965, when the design of interiors, cars, fashion and architecture was quite progressive, fuelled by the optimism and renewed zest for living after World War Two. The heart of mid-century modern home design was 'structural transparency', a simple construction style using large expanses of floor-to-ceiling glass to allow in the natural light. The style was pared-back, inexpensive, functional and modern; open to the environment, with a great sense of place.

We like to mix that style with elements from other eras to provide a further dimension. We mix the raw with the refined and sometimes blend colours, while at other times we choose contrasting combinations that give a feeling of spirited spontaneity. It is all wrapped up in a bundle that is very connected to the outdoors.

A feeling of comfort and warmth, as seen in Jamie's Sydney home, is created with a mix of outdoor organic and natural elements, such as timber, leather, jute, wool, copper and fire, used indoors.

SPATIAL AWARENESS

There is a reason why the most successful interiors work, and it's not just because of the colours used or the way they are decorated. That is important, of course, but if you strip it all away, what you are left with are simply four walls, a ceiling, the orientation to the light and the space's potential. The most important factor is the spatial design, namely the positioning of all these elements.

It's the distance between the walls and the space within, that once organised, divided and furnished, encourages conversation and provides a sense of security or intimacy. It's the height of the ceiling that can lift our spirits as we enter a room. Frank Lloyd Wright was the master of accentuating this with his 'compression release' technique, which involved making some spaces in a building small and others more expansive, re-creating the feeling you get in nature itself – a sensation of opening up to the natural world.

I have seen this technique illustrated in many dwellings he designed, including his winter school, Taliesen West, in Phoenix, Arizona, a real treat for any creative person to visit. He deliberately shrinks the portal or doorway, accentuating the size of the room. When you move from a confined space into a more expansive one it gives you a lovely sensation, as if you are moving through a dense, dark forest into a clearing of soft grass, wildflowers and dappled sunlight. So simple yet so powerful. I have mimicked this technique on many occasions.

The Elrod House is circular in form and the spatial plan is quite different from the rectilinear configurations traditionally used in modern architecture and interior design. Because of this, the furnishings seem to travel organically through the home's interior.

COLOUR

One of the pure joys of my work life is working with colour. I love all colours, from shades of white and neutrals through to muddy and muted, from pastel gelatos to crisp brights, right through to iridescents and fluoros. I enjoy working with the whole spectrum and, as always, am inspired by Mother Nature and the way she plays with colour.

There are endless combinations of tones and shades of colour in nature, so the ways in which you can express yourself are limitless. There are subtle changes in shading that are so pretty and peaceful, but also outright contrast 'smash-the-Ming-vase', shocking moments when incredible colours collide.

I don't understand why so many people are afraid to play with colour – and that's just what you're doing, playing. It's so much fun decorating and living with different colours and changing them every so often. We shouldn't take design too seriously. I like to be spontaneous when it comes to colour choice and not to agonise about it too much, otherwise fear starts to creep in and I end up back-tracking. It takes practice to trust your first response to colour – be bold, be childlike and play around a bit. The colours you live with should put a smile on your dial.

Natural materials and fibres can help to balance more intense colours. Heavier elements such as wooden furniture, woollen rugs, animal hides and skins, linens, silks, cottons and other natural objects can also help to 'ground' or balance the flighty colours in a scheme. The addition of patina and texture has a similar effect.

We are all consciously and subconsciously drawn to certain colours. If you are, then use them, for goodness sake! You're meant to – that's why you're drawn to them in the first place. Colour is one of the simplest and most economical ways to refresh an interior. It's an essential design tool.

In my team we work with a larger, master palette that will always have neutrals, warm and cool colours. The brightness and shade of the colours will evolve from season to season depending on trends in fashion and lifestyle, and so on. From this master palette, we create smaller, more focused colour palettes, drawing on one or two striking colours that work well together. Sometimes, we might use several shades of one colour. We would almost always add one or two neutrals to the mix and then the 'random' rebel colour that keeps the palette edgy.

Here's an example of how we do it:

For a really fun, fresh colour scheme, we've pulled all the shades of green from the master palette and colour-matched them to Porter's Paints colours Evergreen, Banana Leaf, Wild Moss and Granny Smith. We've then added a light grey called Bachiotto Grey (the neutral shade) and a zingy, acid yellow called Lemongrass.

Several years ago we started our first interior collection with rugs inspired by images from nature, such as where the sea fades into the sky or the clouds fade into the dense green foliage. This collection was called Horizon and I believe the reason it has been so successful – it has been going for years – is because of its gradation of colours, which allows the designer or homeowner to match something in the room from one of the colours of the spectrum by tying in a sense of place for the rug.

This is just one example of how you can play with colour. There's an endless array of combinations you can try. Choosing colours is a process of feeling your way through. It is always evolving, because it is a very spontaneous thing. So, for instance, the choice of different shades of green shown here was inspired by driving down a tree-lined street with various foliage colours on display through bright, dappled sunlight.

OUR FURNITURE DESIGN: THE FIRST STEPS, LED BY NATURE

My first foray into furniture design was by necessity, when we couldn't source furniture to fit the spaces we had designed for private homes and hotels. For one client I designed a table that seated twenty-five using seven types of recycled timber, giving the table an eclectic and environmentally responsible feel.

Another time, I set about designing a series of stools inspired by nature. The Ficus stool is based on the butt of a fig tree. You can see here from its early sketches that it is derived from the aggressive above-ground root system that fig trees have to stabilise their heavy canopies. Then we developed the Bungalow collection, with a series of tapered, bone-like legs, soft rounded corners and a woven leather top. This style has been extremely successful and has now morphed into more than twenty spin-off designs. I believe the secret to its success is that there are no straight lines, yet the structure and engineering is reliable and the form seems well connected to the earth and somewhat related to the human body.

I think that the best way to illustrate my interior design style is to give you a peek into my homes in Los Angeles and Sydney. Although they are different in many ways, they do have a number of similarities. Both can be described as natural modern interiors with a strong connection to the outdoors.

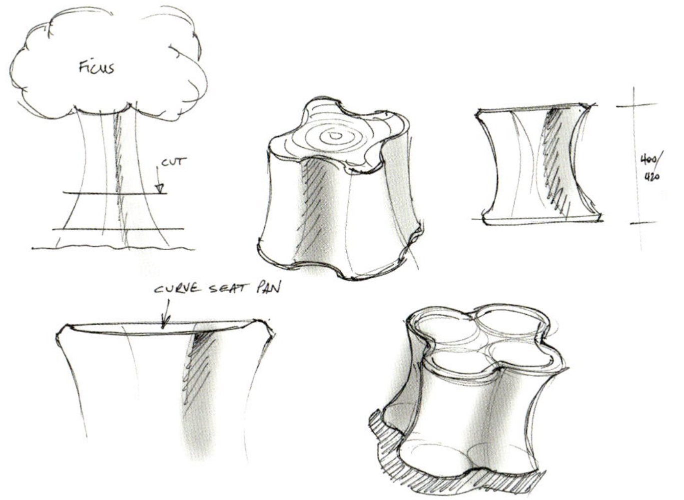

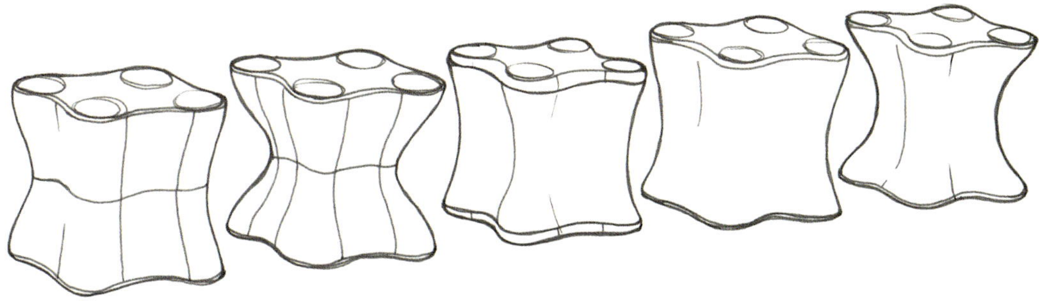

I've always had a fascination with the buttress roots of the large shallow-rooted Moreton Bay fig trees found around Sydney. These huge roots do not penetrate the deeper levels of soil, yet they prevent the tree from falling over, hence the name 'buttress'.

These buttress roots were the inspiration for the concept of the Ficus Stool which I designed for Riva 1920. We began the creative process by photographing many different fig trees and their roots. Then we began sketching a stylised section of the root and morphing the shape until we arrived at something that was pleasing to the eye and would be comfortable to sit on too. We chose cedar to express this design.

CREATING THE BUNGALOW COLLECTION

What can I say? I like the shape of bones and think they look interesting. As a kid I liked to watch *The Flintstones* too! This was the springboard inspiration concept behind our whole Bungalow collection.

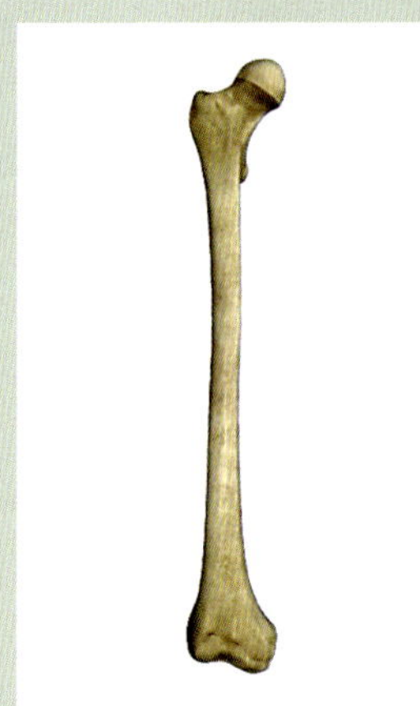

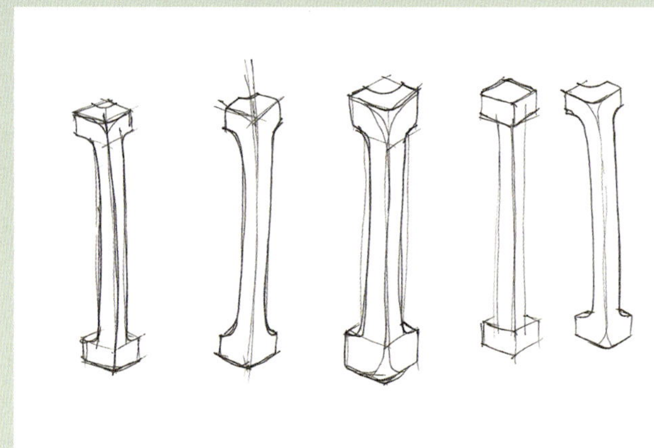

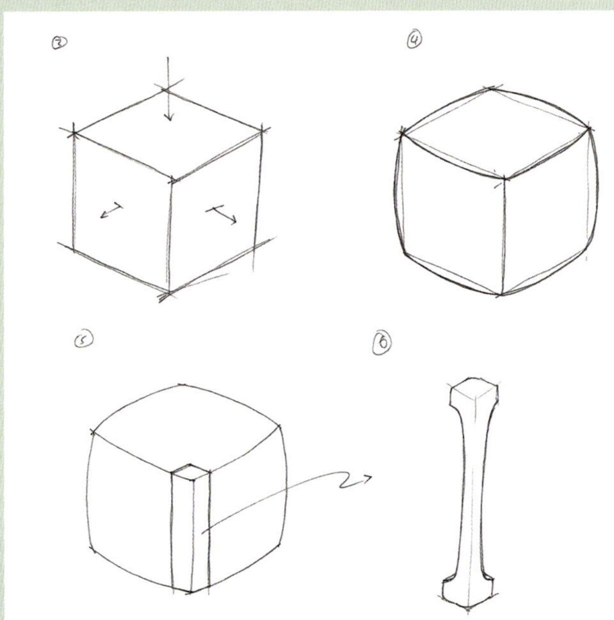

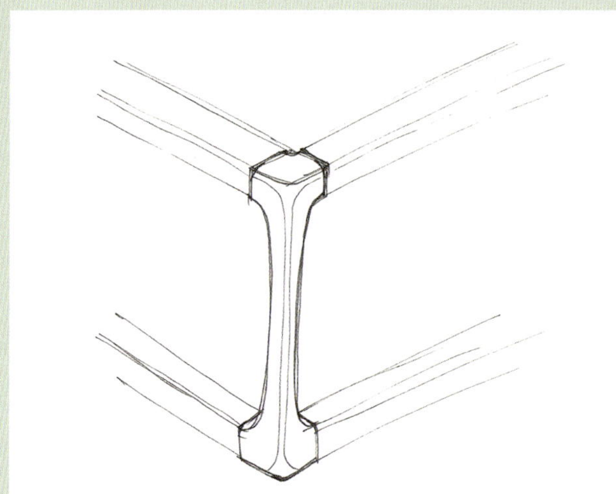

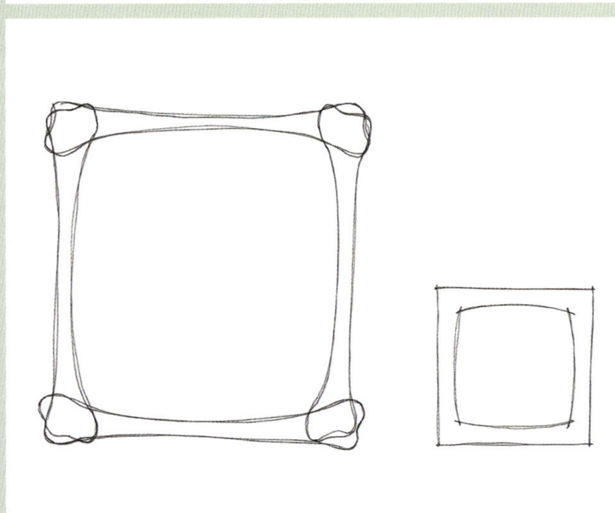

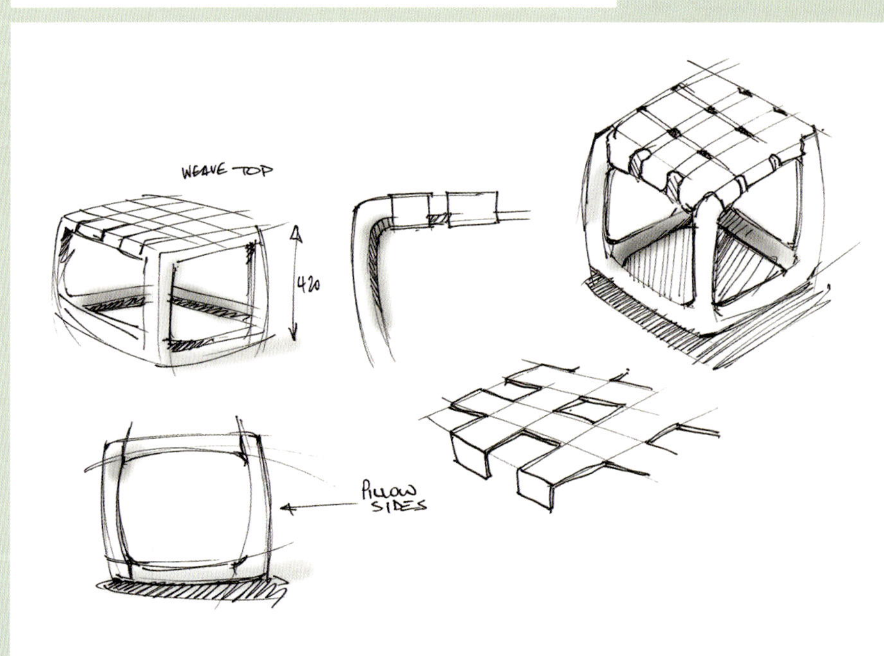

As with the Ficus Stool, we began by playing around with the shape of bones, making various sketches and then stylising those shapes, knowing we were going to be working in American walnut. We repeated the shapes and worked out how each one would connect to the other to create a support frame.

The Bungalow collection consists of a single stool, a three-seater bench and a single armchair. It is upholstered with luxurious Italian woven leather straps, and matching cushions.

JAMIE'S HOME
LOS ANGELES

JAMIE'S HOME: LOS ANGELES

Working in Los Angeles for long periods of time, far away from Australia, left me yearning for my own patch of dirt to scratch around in while I was in the USA. I have always been a fan of mid-century modern architecture and found myself a gem of a house in the hills of Hollywood. The house and garden definitely needed some TLC, but where most people would have seen the tricky terrain of the site as limiting, I saw it as an exciting challenge. This was the first garden I had designed for myself and I finally had the opportunity to 'walk the talk' when it came to my design philosophy.

My main design objective with this house was to extend the interior of the house outward into the outdoor space in a seamless continuum, to create what we call 'transterior' harmony, which I discuss later in the book. I also wanted the interior design to incorporate natural materials and earthy, organic colours and textures.

The reason I love mid-century modern architecture so much is that it exemplifies the best of transterior living. Houses in this style have integrated indoor-outdoor spaces with floor-to-ceiling windows, where the garden rushes up to meet you, letting in fresh air and sunshine to lift your spirits and improve your health and wellbeing.

The Studio

My home office/design studio is like a contemporary tree house, drenched in dappled light. Nowhere on the property is the connection to nature as great as it is here. I designed this dwelling in collaboration with Modern-Shed, a small American architecture firm that provides innovative, eco-friendly solutions to lack of space. We call it 'the greenhouse' and it sits

My design studio perched in the Hollywood Hills of LA is totally transterior. Sunlight floods the interior space because I literally pulled the walls apart with vertical ribbons of glazing in between each wall panel. There is even a grid of glazing where the walls meet the ceiling for maximum exposure to the garden beyond.

SOURCE BOOK
jamie durie
JAMIE DURIE
OUTSIDE
OUTDOOR

on top of the garage. I have always thought it would be a good idea to design a greenhouse for people as well as plants, to give them another room to decorate and inhabit – one with enough natural light to service their plants as well.

Plants and humans both want the same thing from their living environments: natural light and ventilation. There is something especially nice about spending time in a space originally designed mainly for plants.

The interior design of this newly built space needed to be consistent with the original home, which was built around 1952. I hand-picked the furniture from estate sales and mid-century modern furniture dealers in Palm Springs. The furniture looks bold in front of the backdrop of vertical windows that I positioned at regular intervals to punch a consistent flood of light into the tree-surrounded dwelling, inviting the vivid green landscape into the room. Alternating with the windows are panels of the same scale in knot-free pine trimmed in cedar – a nod to the zen-inspired cedar architraves used in Japan to frame the view of lush greenery.

Japanese architecture was a great influence on Frank Lloyd Wright and many of the other great architects at the beginning of the last century, from Greene & Greene and Rudolph Schindler right through to many of the mid-century greats like Lautner and even Neutra, so the hint of this in the architecture of my design studio helps to connect it to the main house.

The lighting in the studio is all indirect (by choice), with the main light being cast vertically, creating an illusion of stretching the ceiling height and mimicking the verticality of the windows and wooden panels. A few pieces of vintage art in red macramé, thick, rich oil paintings and one of our own interior rugs, from a collection inspired by the beautiful oyster plant (*Acanthus mollis*), all help to bring the outside in, making my studio luxurious, and typical of our interior design aesthetic.

The Home

Inside the house, the two bedrooms are separated by an internal garden. The master bedroom has large pivoting doors lined with our vertical garden

The bedroom and bath spaces are connected and each flows onto a garden area as well. The interior and exterior dissolve to create a new dimension – the transterior.

PATIO
PATIO
JAMIE DURIE
inspired
Jamie Durie's The Outdoor Room
JAMIE DURIE OUTSIDE

There's nothing better than sitting inside your home and seeing sunlight spill across the floor or look through the windows to watch the magical sight of wind blowing in the trees or hear and see a bird.

blankets, which are filled with plants. The doors open inwardly onto an intimate oasis, dragging the vertical garden wall behind them into the bedroom interior. This has several benefits: a strong, geometrical framed view, a seamless connection to the garden, an extended natural bedroom and meditation area and a garden that seems to creep into the home.

I have designed a Japanese cedar bathtub so that I can bathe outside in my own secluded courtyard full of tropical plants wrapped in a tub built from nature itself.

An outside bath is a traditional part of the typical Japanese *ryokan* bath house experience, where the tubs are made of cedar for a number of reasons, including the fact that the timber expands and contracts. The timber is left in its natural state and finely sanded so it feels warm and luxurious to the touch – it really is a sensory piece. Cedar also has natural antibacterial qualities, and its fragrance, one that is associated with luxury spas, is very appealing and is good for cleansing the sinuses and lungs.

Inside, next to the master bedroom, there is a raised timber deck with a sunken timber bath at the edge of an interior courtyard garden. The inspiration for my bedroom and bathroom came from my travels to Japan, Bali and other Asian resort destinations over the years.

In the living room, original stone detailing around the fireplace brings a beautiful, earthy quality to the interior. The fireplace is flanked on both sides by floor-to-ceiling windows that invite the dense garden into the room. The adjacent wall is made of sliding glass doors that open completely to extend the living room to the swimming pool and daybed pavilions, making the whole space feel very much like a modern resort-style home.

I have incorporated greenery into the architecture, with every room of the house connected to the outdoors. The materials used in the interior spill into the outdoor rooms and vice versa, as the interiors are transformed into a garden house through the integration of plants – the internal garden between the two bedrooms, and the many indoor plants, including fiddle-leaf fig (*Ficus lyrata*), bromeliads, ferns, Spanish moss and orchids.

The Garden

The garden has become my ultimate outdoor room. I have turned the house inside out by creating spaces outside for all aspects of living. I challenged myself to re-create interior rooms outside, to truly deliver the quintessential 'outdoor room'. The lounge room surrounding the firepit and the daybed pavilions are a nod to Palm Springs, and this is the ultimate chill-out zone.

The garden is fully furnished, and organised into conversational settings – what I call destination design or 'build it and they will come'. The more comfortable and inspiring the area, the longer people linger; every aspect of life can be enhanced by a connection to the great outdoors.

I designed the function and architecture of each space – the dining, lounge and kitchen – then abundantly planted all available spaces. I pushed the garden up the walls, using our vertical garden blanket planting system filled with textured, spillover, flowering, scented and even edible plants. This is where our blankets were tested and prototyped.

With backyards getting smaller and homes getting bigger, we need to maximise outdoor living space. It's a matter of replicating the feeling of indoor comfort outside in the form of walls of plants. Taking advantage of vertical space may increase your growing area by up to 40 per cent.

The cosy dining room area has a fireplace and rooftop garden where you can sun yourself in privacy. I have also placed small troughs full of plants into the hollow vertical beams on top of the daybed pavilions. As you can see, I'm not one to leave any hard surface untouched by nature.

Using the hillside terrain to my advantage, I have created terraced vegetable and herb beds that protect the garden from erosion. These supply me with fresh produce; I get about nine kilograms of seedless grapes and thirteen kilograms of plums each year, plus pumpkins, apples, figs, carrots, beet, corn, watermelon, basil, chives, rosemary and chocolate mint.

The outdoor kitchen is in front of this edible garden, beside the dining area, with a long counter and integrated barbecue. You can pick fresh herbs and toss them into iced drinks or onto the barbecue as you cook. The counter is surrounded by bar stools – it's a great place to enjoy sunset cocktails and a chat, and the chef always feels a part of the action.

JULIUS SHULMAN
MODERNISM
REDISCOVERED
JAMIE DURIE
PATIO
inspired
Jamie Durie's The Outdoor Room
JAMIE DURIE OUTSIDE

GET THE LOOK

Introduce the colours of nature inside with your choice of paint, tiles, soft furnishings and decoration.

Bring the textures of nature inside as well by using natural, organic materials such as timber, stone and pebbles.

Another way to introduce nature and an alfresco feeling indoors is to choose nature motifs for wallpaper and fabrics, rugs and blinds.

Outdoors, decoration and soft furnishings are the finishing touches that make all the difference.

Whether it's for alfresco dining or an outdoor conversation setting, the furnishings, lighting and rugs, and the way they are arranged, will affect how easy the space is to use and how good it feels.

100 CONTEMPORARY GREEN BUILDINGS
100 CONTEMPORARY GREEN BUILDINGS
FOOD OF THE WORLD
LUNUGANGA
OF CONTEMPORARY WORLD ARCHITECTURE

JAMIE'S HOME SYDNEY

JAMIE'S HOME: SYDNEY

This house is all about plants on every level, from the ground floor up; not just outside, but also growing out of the lounge room floor, or at kitchen windows. The entire dwelling is a conversation with nature. Some people enter the space and say it feels as if they are on a beautiful yacht, others say it reminds them of a tree house from their childhood; whatever the feeling, it conjures up the experience of being close to nature.

For me, demolishing the '70s beach shack on the Northern Beaches peninsula so I could start from scratch was a dream come true. Loving challenges, I wasn't fazed by the fact that I was facing another tricky terrain. The block of land sits on a blustering escarpment with the most knock-your-socks-off view of the Pacific Ocean to the horizon on two sides.

Even though my brief for the house was to make it as transterior as possible, merging elements of the interior and exterior, we had to make sure we protected the back from the buffeting winds, because it is perched on top of a ridge exposed to the harsh seaside elements. At the same time, I wanted to maintain the connection through to the outside when the weather permitted.

Walter Barda and I created a house that looks from the outside like a jungle-covered fortress, but its organic interior has a womb-like structure that is warm and inviting, like the interior of a luxurious timber yacht that has been shipwrecked, washed ashore at world's end and, over time, has been reclaimed by the earth.

DESTINATION ART
LUXE
MODERNES GARTENDESIGN

Maintaining a simple range of materials and colours in the interior was done mindfully, creating a sense of calm and serenity. This allows plants, artworks and other focal points to jump out and grab your attention.

We've used a few clever tricks to make the most of open-plan living. The glass gaps between walls and ceiling maximise access to daylight and really enhance the feeling of space and light. Open-plan areas can be kept interesting by changing levels, creating bridges, sleeping nooks and balconies for outdoor access.

The Home

I have re-created here the same indoor and outdoor bathrooms I have in my LA home. The master bedroom is open-plan and integrated with the bathroom, which features a deep cedar Japanese tub. The outdoor bath here has been hand-carved from solid granite by artisans in Bali.

The master bedroom, guest bedroom, bathrooms and home office all connect to the mezzanine hallway, which feels a bit like a bridge because it overlooks the living room on the floor below. All the bedrooms and the home office open up onto balcony gardens. The caged timber staircase spans all five levels of the house, and eventually leads to the crow's nest of my 'Chateau Plateau' (as my friends like to call the house) rooftop. This space architecturally replicates the skeletal lines of a whale's ribcage, with a bench seat that runs all the way along one side. At the furthest point it lurches out like the pointy bow of a ship over the most magnificent sweeping views across Bilgola Beach and the coastline.

The way light enters the interior makes the space look a bit like a painting. The light is not bold or glary which, given the proximity to vast expanses of sea and sky, it could have been. Walter and I designed the house so that sunlight enters with a mellow softness, allowing for shadowy places that are integral to the whole aesthetic, which is again very Japanese. The whole house has a *wabi sabi* vibe – a Japanese concept that is difficult to translate, but essentially means the art of finding beauty in the grace, subtlety and patina of natural materials. Interiors are moody and muted, dimly lit in the evenings. The space feels warm and comfortable.

The main living area is split-level, perfect for entertaining, with a sunken lounge in the centre. Outside, there is a lush, floor-to-ceiling garden wall that feels integrated with the interior space, whether the enormous glass sliding doors are open or closed. This vertical garden spans two floors of the house. The mezzanine floor above the living area has a bridge-like hallway that overlooks the sunken living room and garden wall.

The garden steps inside the lounge room with two *Ficus lyrata* (fiddle-leaf fig) trees growing out of the floor, and a mixture of mondo grass, anthuriums, maidenhair ferns and orchids under their branches.

The dirt in these gardens goes through the foundations into the earth, helping to ground the house, as well as grounding everyone in the house.

The open-plan kitchen is above the sunken living area, overlooking the whole floor like a captain's lookout – it is definitely the heart of the house. A large timber island bench houses the stove top and is the perfect breakfast bar. There are sky-blue perspex troughs growing a myriad of herbs and lettuces along the window ledge, framing the ocean views.

Outdoors

The outdoor area leading from the kitchen level is a different layout, featuring a wet-edge swimming pool, spa and carp pond. Certain aspects of the interior design are mirrored, as this outdoor room is also split-level, with a sunken lounge. It's not a huge area, but it can be used for a range of activities: lounging on a daybed, cooking in an outdoor kitchen with all mod cons or dining at a table which resembles a yacht's deck. It is all integrated with plants, of course, and you can also swim, sun yourself on a deckchair beside the pool, gather around a firepit in a sunken conversation pit or recline on the lawn. I have drawn on the spectrum of my outdoor room design philosophies and poured them all into my dream home.

On the northern side of the house a bright room juts out into the front garden jungle. It's so protected and private you would never know it was the street side. The walls open up on three sides, with one side merging onto a terraced bonsai plant gallery. The jungle outdoor room holds my precious plant collection – amazing plants I've been collecting over a long period of time, such as my beloved *Dracaena draco* (dragon tree), *Brachychiton rupestris* (Queensland bottle tree), *Chorisia speciosa* (kapok tree) and my *Aloe bainesii* (tree aloe), to name just a few.

Although I've now sold this beautiful home, I had so much joy creating it with Walter and Nadine. It is truly a garden house where the essence of the natural landscape is embraced wholeheartedly, at one with the architecture and interior design. I felt that it was time to move on to my next project and let someone else enjoy it.

ENVIRONMENTAL ASPECTS

It is amazing in this day and age that we are still using drinking water to water our plants, and are not using solar energy more. I have tried in my own homes to include as many sustainable features as possible.

Greywater system to harvest the water from the basins, showers and washing machine. Water is filtered on site for a maximum of 72 hours then used to irrigate the gardens.

Rainwater harvested from the zinc roof is collected in the channel in the centre, then stored under the front lawn and used to irrigate the property and for other purposes such as the flushing of toilets.

The house features several solar 'passive design' techniques – meaning features that ensure that the house is naturally warmer in winter and cooler in summer, reducing the need for auxiliary heating or cooling.

- The vertical greenwall blanket provides passive climate control of the interior.

- The butterfly-style roof, the structure of which was inspired by seagull wings, runs north to south, allowing passive climate control inside as cool air created from the greenwall comes in, and heat escapes through ventilation in the roof.

- The layout allows for passive airflow and circulation throughout the home by intelligent room orientation. Well-positioned openings encourage airflow and circulation.

We used recycled timbers for the central columns, and sustainable blackbutt elsewhere in floors, kickboards and architraves for fire safety.

Only two levels of the house are above the existing ground level. The rest I submerged into the ground to integrate it into the topography. I used the excavated sandstone in the gabion baskets which provide natural filtration of rainwater throughout the site.

The planting has been integrated with the architecture to create seamless indoor/outdoor flow and enhance climate control.

Natural materials such as the cedar wood bath provide therapeutic aromatherapy and rejuvenation.

Solar panels on the roof provide energy for the home.

The design of the timber roof is inspired by the rib cage of a southern right whale. The roof's ribs expand out towards the ocean where, in the right season, you can see pods of up to thirty whales.

The butterfly roof is the perfect shape for collecting rainwater.

In the designs for our clients as well as in my private homes we always strive to create the greatest connection to nature. On top of using the most sustainable building practices and materials, we pay homage to nature in the design of the building, the interior and the furniture. We also introduce natural materials, open up the space where the room meets the garden and blend the architecture into the topography.

OUR TRANSTERIOR DESIGN PHILOSOPHY

WHAT DOES 'TRANSTERIOR' MEAN?

'Transterior' is a term Nadine and I have coined to describe the space where the interior and exterior of a home merge. Our aim has always been to create a seamless transition between the two – to take the indoors out and bring the outside in, creating a greater connection to nature. What you get is a blurred line, where a strong sense of shared space evokes an alfresco feeling, which reflects the quintessential Australian lifestyle.

This transterior space is often the threshold where architecture meets nature, such as where a verandah or sliding doors open onto a courtyard or garden. You can, however, create the same feeling in a room without that physical threshold by bringing nature indoors through your choice of natural, handmade organic materials, textures and colours.

What we are trying to do is to re-create the outdoors vibe indoors, because we believe that everything feels better outside – lounging, dining, cooking, sleeping or chatting to your friends and family. We want you to feel just as good inside as you do outside.

I love watching people's jaws drop as they walk into my living room and discover that the fourth wall is a six-metre living wall embedded with hand-selected tropical plants. There's an element of surprise and life force generated by having plants vertically installed as part of your living space.

By the same token, you can create outdoor rooms within a garden that are as comfortable and luxurious as any interior room. I call this 'luxescaping'. The more luxurious something looks and feels, the more it feels like 'forbidden fruit' when it is taken outside. I'm talking rugs, cushions, plush drapes and fabrics, chandeliers, artworks – whatever your heart desires. Most of my clients say, 'Can I really have this outside?' and that is the exact response to design that drives me.

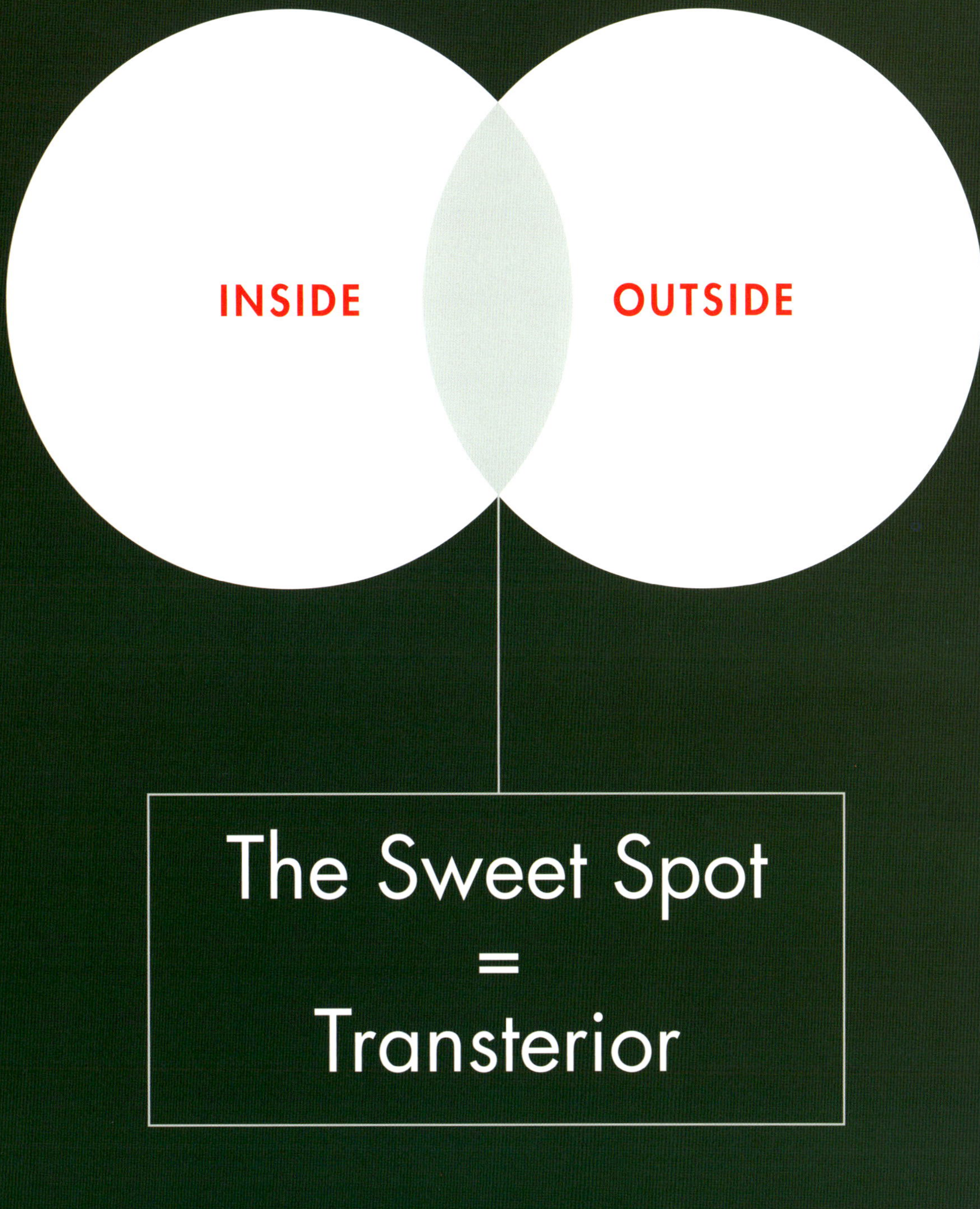
INSIDE
OUTSIDE
The Sweet Spot
=
Transterior

The challenge comes from finding materials durable enough to last outside, but these days we are able to break down many barriers thanks to advances in technology, so let's make the most of every opportunity to take interior elements outside.

To create a transterior, the trick is to pull as many features as possible from the exterior into the interior and vice versa, exchanging materials, textures, colours and even lights, so the two spaces become one – the ultimate goal.

The relationship between people and plants is paramount. My whole career has been anchored around facilitating that connection. For more than a decade, I've dedicated myself to finding new ways to say, 'Let's go outside', designing outdoor living rooms, dining rooms, bathrooms, kitchens and even bedrooms. These days, there is nothing that can't be done outdoors – even showering outside feels more sacred. Outside is where we spend precious, quality downtime with our family and friends – it's here that unforgettable memories are made.

What matters is that by extending inside living outwards, and vice versa, bringing elements of the outside indoors, we're reconnecting with the natural world. I believe this is vital to our sense of wellbeing.

On the following pages are some great illustrations of the transterior concept, in built form, in Australia and overseas. It's no secret that we all want to be closer to nature, and designers, architects and manufacturers all over the world are responding to that need. The examples vary, but what I've noticed in my travels is that sometimes the countries with the least opportunities for outdoor living come up with the best types of innovation or design, which totally quench your thirst for a natural connection.

The transterior movement is gaining momentum as more and more of us want to spend a greater amount of time outdoors with all the creature comforts of interior luxury, while simultaneously enjoying elements of raw, outdoor luxury inside our homes, as seen in this home in Amagansett on Long Island, New York.

BIRCHGROVE HOUSE

Sydney, Australia

This wonderful example of a transterior space by Nobbs Radford Architecture illustrates how nature can intersect with architecture. You can completely retract the glass sliding doors, so the whole interior opens up to the outdoor courtyard, letting the sunlight and fresh air in. You can see how the natural world spills into the interior – the kitchen, dining and living room become one with the outside.

BV HOUSE

Porto Feliz, Brazil

This house in Brazil by Biselli Katchborian reinforces the connection with the outdoors in two ways – by planting indoors to create an interior garden behind the dining table, and by designing the outer so that it echoes the indoor lounge and dining room. Another option when bringing plants inside if the natural light is limited is to swap the plants out on a three-week rotation.

Skylights are useful, and here you see how the architect has cleverly allowed natural light to spill over the interior walls and even bounce off the reflection of the lacquered wood to feed light into the planters. Substitute lighting can also help – the best substitutes for natural light are hydroponic lights, which usually need to be on for at least six hours each day to keep the plants healthy. Be careful because they can use a lot of power, so try LED lights and/or solar-power panels to cancel out your additional power requirements.

GUARUJÁ BEACH HOUSE

Guarujá, Brazil

When the barrier between inside and out is glazing, it's hardly an obstruction. This house is a great case in point of how this astonishing vista naturally becomes an instrinsic part of the interior experience as well.

LONG COURTYARD HOUSE

Alexandria, Australia

Scale Architecture have really integrated the indoors with the outdoors in this home. This is even more apparent when the doors are open. What helps to blur the lines is the transfer of building materials between spaces. Concrete render on the fences is matched by a polished concrete floor and kitchen bench. Exterior bricks have become the feature backdrop for the kitchen wall, and, finally, polished wooden eaves are used on the exterior to add a sense of luxury to the outdoors.

CHELSEA TOWNHOUSE

London, England

I love the fact that there is no delineation between the interior and exterior of this Chelsea townhouse by Alison Henry – this is a classic example of how to unify living spaces in a seamless way. Although there is a subtle difference in the materials used, because the outdoor furniture needs to be able to weather the elements, the same colour palette and sense of luxury and comfort are apparent in both the indoor and outdoor furniture.

The animal fur and phalaenopsis orchids have brought nature inside but, even more cleverly, the selection of white furniture both indoors and out makes it feel like one large room. We like to say, 'Their lounge room just got a whole lot bigger.'

MOSMAN HOUSE

Sydney, Australia

Seamless glass windows deliver the greatest floor-to-ceiling views, allowing the light and reflection of outdoors to bounce off the polished floors. Sheer drapes help with the glare without creating a disconnection between the interior and outside worlds.

ANANDA LAKE HOUSE

The Catskills, Upstate New York

New York-based Aussie photographer James Houston is one of our best friends. With his Scottish-born restaurateur partner, Brian McGrory, he bought a block of land on a lake in the Catskill Mountains, two hours' drive from Manhattan. It feels like Scotland – in fact on the sales brochure it was even captioned 'Just like Scotland'.

‘The word “Ānanda” means bliss in Sanskrit and some other Indian languages. When designing the house, the goal was to create an inspiring open living space that connected the interior with the natural environment. I wanted a retreat that felt like an exclusive spa, somewhere to escape the intense energy of Manhattan and to connect with nature.’

JAMES HOUSTON

ANANDA LAKE HOUSE

There was a lot of serendipity involved for James and Brian in finding the land, then designing and building the house. James remembers, 'It really was a wonderful process . . . It was a twist of fate – things kept falling into our laps.'

The house is built close to the lake and is surrounded by woodland, with no other houses in sight. The design was a collaboration between James, Brian, architect Jonathan Marvel and Shuji Suzumori, a Japanese architect who brought an international influence to the design.

I consulted on the garden, giving some friendly advice to my mates by suggesting that the odd tree and boulder be built into the surrounding decking to ensure the lines between landscape and architecture truly overlapped. One of the nicest aspects of the landscape is an intimate conversation setting arranged around an open firepit bowl perfectly positioned near the edge of the tranquil lake.

It is a quintessential 'transterior' design – nature and materials have been perfectly synthesised. The mix of timber and stone, glass and steel give the house its natural, organic atmosphere. Ananda is a blend of Japanese zen-minimalism, Australian beach house and *On Golden Pond* lake house. It feels comfortable and unpretentious, yet evokes a sense of luxury akin to a resort-style spa.

The key thing was to position the house on the block so as to maximise the meditative view facing south over the lake, with pine trees all around. Everywhere you look the outdoors is drawn in through innovative and imaginative interior design. The husk of the house includes a lot of timber and stone, with generous spans of glazing to engage the outlook onto the surrounding forest and lake. The warm, raw, luxurious furnishings in wood, leather and fur work together with an earthy colour palette to

James Houston believes there is a direct correlation between your headspace and your homespace. 'It has taken me many years to develop my design aesthetic and work out the environment I need to have around me in order to be really inspired and motivated,' he says.

intensify the outdoorsy air of the house. The enclosing woodland seems to be rushing up to meet you through the sweeping windows and doorways.

'You can lie in the bathtub in the main bathroom and watch the full moon come up,' says James. The open-plan rooms flow from one to the other and while each has a distinct feel and character, they make up the whole seamlessly.

Furnishings are organic and textural. Fur, leather, suede, natural timbers, linen and wool combine to create a sumptuous palette. The decoration includes a collection of bonsai trees, antlers, crystals, tribal sculptures and tree branches.

Creating this incredible lake house was the first step for James towards realising his dream of creating a design vision that promotes the integration of mind and lifestyle. Here the architects and homeowners shared the same vision, so the house speaks to the land and opens itself up to it at every opportunity, and the interiors do the same by pulling nature inside with every choice.

When it is freezing outside, you can wrap yourself up on this luxurious daybed layered in reindeer pelts and textural fabric cushions and still feel connected to all the change of season's spectacular glory, right beside you.

Colour is one of the main ways to make an impact on the look and feel of the exterior of your house. My favourite exterior colours are those that are most contextual to their environment, blending in seamlessly with the natural landscape, as Ananda does so beautifully.

INSPIRATION IS EVERYWHERE

WHERE TO FIND INSPIRATION

I have always believed that inspiration is everywhere. In terms of my own design process, I can only describe it as an organic thing that just happens, usually during my first meeting or site visit with a client. Something they say or do will trigger something in my own sensory 'hard drive' where I've stored a library of flotsam and jetsam that has inspired me over the years.

There are multiple solutions for any one space and, provided those concepts are carefully considered, functional, balanced and harmonious, no one design is necessarily better than any other. We all have different approaches and ours, like everyone else's, has a unique fingerprint.

After decades on the planet and all the travelling I've done (trust me, I've done *lots* of travelling), I have a lot to draw upon. My bedrock of inspiration is Mother Nature, the ultimate artist, designer, stylist, composer, director. Imagine trying to replicate a body of texture, colour, architecture and composition where no design is ever the same – nature is impossible to rival. Sometimes, though, I've been inspired by a man-made object: an artwork, paint colour, bowl of ice cream or Dolce & Gabbana suit.

You need a point of inspiration as a launching pad for the design process. Mine usually starts with a point of reference connected to nature which inspires me, lights my fire, and gets my creative juices flowing.

It's a three-step thing:

1. **DESIGN INSPIRATION**
2. **DESIGN CONCEPT**
3. **DESIGNED SPACE**

This was once one of the biggest water towers in Europe and is now an amazing 5-star hotel. Standing derelict for many years, the 19th century tower is startling, with beautiful exposed brickwork and an imposing 11-storey entrance foyer. Responsible for the superb interiors, Andrée Putman transformed this utilitarian building into a masterpiece. I love how something as down to earth, sensible and pragmatic as a water tower can be looked at as an arty thing of beauty.

1 DESIGN INSPIRATION

When I took my daughter for walks as a child I would try to teach her to look around all the time – I mean really look closely and notice the elements around her, not just skim over the surface.

We all see things in different ways. If you took two people for a walk down the same street at the same time, each would notice different things. You need to be open to inspiration; it's important to allow yourself time to let your mind wander and to nurture your imagination.

There are no rules about the 'right' inspiration either. It only needs to be true for you – as they say, beauty is in the eye of the beholder. What inspires you stimulates your thoughts and creative activity.

Sometimes I'm inspired by one element, but I look at it broadly – my creative process is to keep drilling down to the essentials until I have a solution I'm satisfied with. Other times, I might be inspired by more than one element, but still take a broad 'mood' perspective, then break down the different qualities and aspects (both literal and abstract) into a design solution.

I'm going to describe how to do this in more detail as we go, so bear with me.

2 DESIGN CONCEPT

For a design concept to work, it should have a beauty that appeals to you, and a theory that explains your reasons for choosing it. The idea is to break the design concept down into its parts: shape, line, texture, colour, scale, proportion, rhythm and movement.

Shape, Space and Form

When I talk about shape, I mean the two-dimensional shape of an object in relation to another nearby object. It can refer to the outline or the shape of the actual piece of furniture or object, or the space itself. Shapes are referred to as being geometric, organic, circular and so on. For example, an ottoman can be a circular shape but multiples of them could be arranged into a geometric shape within a space. It is different to the form of an object because form is more three-dimensional. Forms can be either hollow or solid. A space can be flat and two-dimensional or can have volume and be three-dimensional. If a space is enclosed, it can also be referred to as a 'shape'; however, if it's not contained, it is referred to as 'space'. Space and shape work in tandem to give foreground and background or light and shade to a room.

Line

In interior design, the word 'line' doesn't refer to an actual line; it is something implicit, such as a fashion silhouette or a change of colour in a room. It is an element used to be able to define outlines, shapes and so on, and it is also implied by the edges of shapes and forms. For example, you can refer to a vertical line which could denote columns, curtains, a doorway.

A line can be zigzagged, angled, straight, dotted, flowing and curved, flat or textured. The curve of a staircase has a curved line. A herringbone parquetry floor has a zigzag line. A bank of tall windows with drapes on suggests vertical lines. Painting a chair-rail stripe on the walls of a room creates a horizontal line. You get the idea.

Texture

Every surface has a texture, ranging from rough and jagged, like gravel, through to smooth, like polished chrome. Some textures are inviting, while others repel. Using a mixture of different textures in an interior scheme increases interest and introduces variety.

Textures can be tactile or simple. A tactile texture has a three-dimensional surface, while a simple texture is two-dimensional. For example, a cushion fabric might have a cactus print on it, making the texture look rough, when the surface of the fabric is actually smooth. It is important to use both types of texture in combination, especially with our style of organic, earthy interiors of raw luxury. Texture is key.

Colour

Colour is often described according to its hue (pure colour) or value (lightness or darkness). Colour can have a huge psychological impact, depending on how it is used. We all have an instant response to colour, with certain colours evoking different emotions. People believe that reds, magentas and dark purples can be strong, somewhat angry colours while light blues, yellows and pale greens evoke happiness.

When I am using bright colours I usually complement them with subtle earthy tones which, I find, add a level of balance so the brights are more digestible.

Scale

Scale is the suggested relationship between two or more objects in a space. There are many standardised measurements for the heights of counters, tables, chairs and even step risers, however, it's important to work out what suits you or your client best. I have my favourite standard measurements for certain things.

Maybe it's because I am vertically challenged that I like low-to-the-ground scale furnishings, sunken living rooms and firepits! I like the furniture to be less intrusive and, where possible, built-in or sunken down into level changes as I feel that this 'glues' the furniture to the architecture, making the home feel more considered. It also invites people to settle into the home rather than move pieces around into areas that are not as social.

Proportion

Proportion refers to the relative size of various elements within the design. In a home, the standard of measurement is in relation to the human body, because you want your home to feel cosy and nurturing. In public spaces, the proportion can be scaled up to make the area feel more grand and spacious.

Rhythm and Movement

Rhythm and movement are closely related. Rhythm refers to the movement of your eye in a space where some elements are repeated – the dance of elements within a space. Rhythm and movement can refer to the flow throughout your house or within an individual room. Repetition of certain elements can create the feeling of rhythm in an interior scheme, as can different patterns and textures. Movement is the visual path created for the viewer's eye through space to a particular focal point.

Layers of Design

We begin the design process by brainstorming the essence of the concept and writing the descriptive words on a page. This gives our inspiration some form, some flesh on the bones. From here we then start matching materials and finishes that connect to the words and express them: furniture and light fittings, wallpapers and paints, floor coverings and fabrics all begin to speak the language of the concept.

Next, we collect samples and swatches of fabrics, tiles, carpets, timber, stones, wallpapers, rugs, leather and suede, paints, tear sheets from magazines, pictures from catalogues and pictures of artworks to create a mood board that reflects the feeling that the design concept originally inspired.

As we add the layers of different materials with hard surfaces and then the luxurious elements of furniture, fabrics, rugs, patterns and prints as finishing layers, the space starts to take shape, becoming a more vigorous version of the original inspiration launching pad.

Designing furniture is similar. The brief is dictated by the environment the furniture is destined for. The concept starts with a particular shape or texture derived from a particular form (usually natural). From pencil sketch it goes into a CAD (computer-aided design) program as a line drawing, which we then sculpt and manipulate so that it takes on a set of proportions that will allow that piece of furniture to perform its function.

GASCOIGN
& KING
PADDINGTON

3 DESIGNED SPACE

Once you've chosen your inspiration, then created your design concept, you need to transform those creative concepts into the interior scheme for a room. You need to consider how you would arrange elements within that space – the spatial design.

We apply our inspiration filter to every aspect of the design concept. We collect lots of different materials and then start to exclude the extraneous ones, refining the concept down to its essential elements. Again, this is different for everybody – what is essential for us may not be for you.

I think that the best way for you to understand this is for us to show you how the process unfolds by walking you through the steps. We are going to give you six examples of design inspiration with mood boards showing how we develop a design concept from the initial inspiration. We will then show you an interior that could have been the end product.

EGG

Eggs come in all shapes and sizes, from large, stippled ostrich eggs, charcoal-coloured emu eggs, blue robin and duck eggs to soft, glossy turtle eggs, just to name a few. Here we've juxtaposed the humble chicken eggs that we have for breakfast against the crumpled carton they are nestled into.

pure

simple

zen

natural

organic

EGG

moulded

contrast

CARTON

raw

crumpled

LET'S BREAK IT DOWN

Shape	The egg has fragile curves and a perfect, organic shape. The carton shape is synthetic.
Line	The egg has a natural, smooth, elegant line while the carton has hills and valleys having been moulded into shape.
Texture	The egg has micro-stippling that is barely visible and smooth to the touch, while the carton is raw and crumpled.
Colour	The egg is white through to shades of creamy beige and the carton is greyish-white.
Scale, proportion & balance	The egg is small and neat in scale and balance and bottom-heavy in proportion. The carton has an even proportion and scale, creating a yin/yang balance in the way the eggs nestle into the carton.
Rhythm & movement	The repetition in the arrangement of the eggs in the carton creates harmony.
Core feeling	SIMPLE, NATURAL

Mood board

- natural leather
- cowhide
- bamboo
- weathered and limed timber
- whitewashed timber-look tile
- pale ceramic tiles in matt, gloss and crackle glazes
- textured knits
- crushed linens and cottons
- transparent muslins
- chunky woven rug in natural fibre
- string macramé
- mother of pearl
- rusted wire
- paints in different shades of white and shell

DESIGNED SPACE

Virgine Batterson owns mamapapa, a beautiful clothing shop on Sydney's Northern Beaches. This rustic retreat is a sublime example of a natural interior design palette, with a juxtaposition of smooth and textural materials and finishes.

The simple room's only adornments are elements from nature such as dried branches, a cowhide rug, a string of humble calico bunting and found objects of rusty wire. There is little to distract the eye and the white-on-white-on-cream palette is soothing and calm.

Paola Navone's Ghost sofa, designed for Gervasoni, is my all-time favourite comfy sofa. I love its extreme simplicity, dressed in loose slipcovers of crumpled white linen. Heaven. This casual chameleon of the upholstered furniture world can be dressed up or down depending on which cushions and throws you toss on it. I love relaxed, uncontrived furniture like this.

In every corner there is a perfect still life arrangement that rivals the idiosyncratic poetry of a Morandi painting. The space is almost monastic, with a patina of age, yet a seriously contemporary, rustic take on beach-style modernity.

'I wanted to maintain the charm of the house,' says Virgine. 'I love many features but needed to add my personal touch to make it come alive for me.' As soon as she and her family moved in they ripped out all the carpeting and painted all the walls white. They would make do with that for the moment.

'I love simple and white, all branches, leaves ... anything with texture, old, natural, a mix of materials,' says Virgine. 'I am always changing things.' I am inspired by her beautiful, styled vignettes at every turn. The space is so creative with a magical innocence and is charming to be in.

SALT & PEPPER

White sea salt, pink Himalayan salt and black pepper are separate ingredients which, incombination, become something beautiful and new.

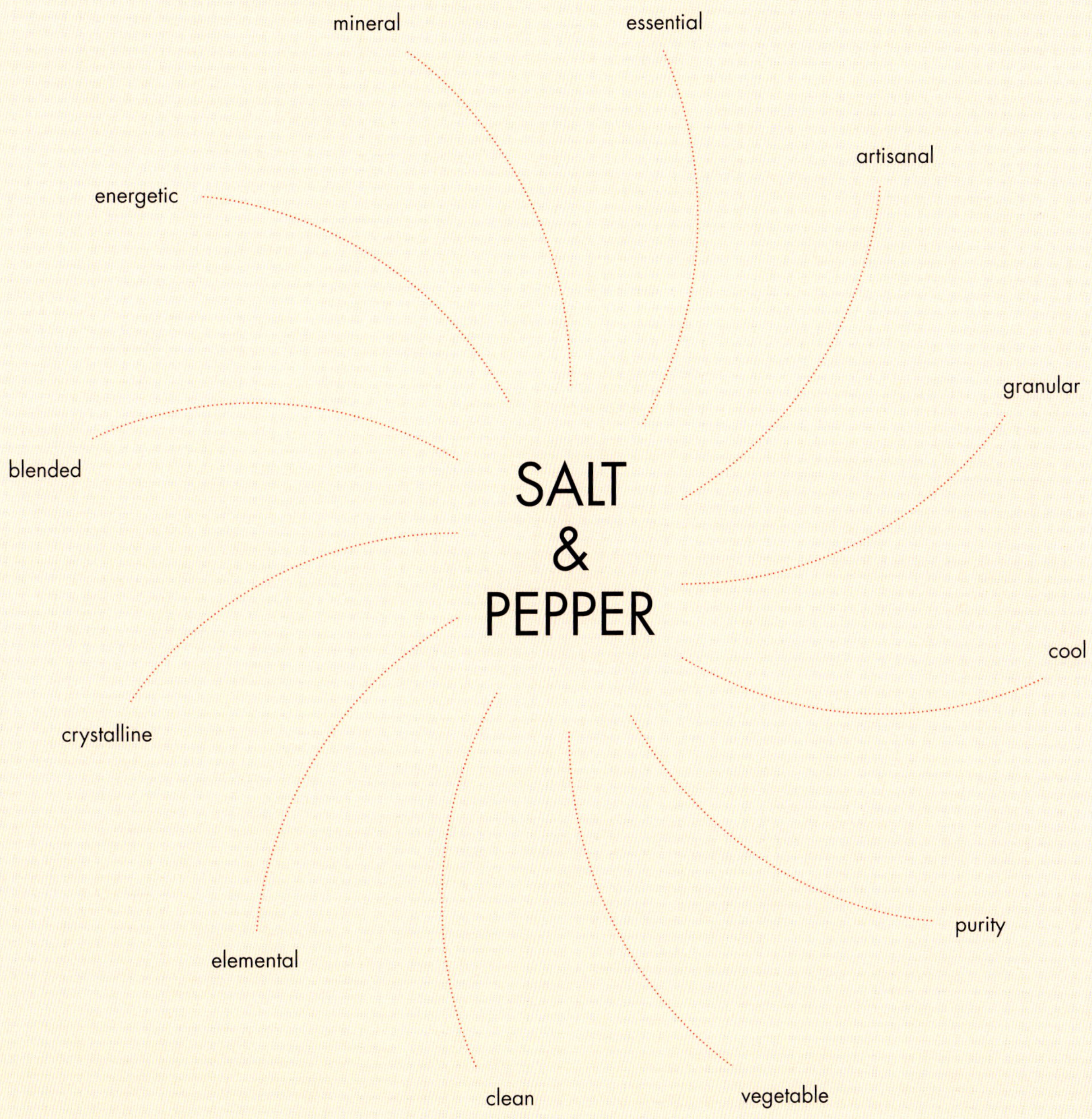

LET'S BREAK IT DOWN

Shape	Separate, individual elements that have been grouped together and work well to create a blended new entity. The soft rounded shapes of the furnishings fit together in a harmonious grouping.
Line	Seamless as one element merges with the other. Primarily the arrangement of the room follows a horizontal line, which always creates the most peaceful and calm atmosphere in a room.
Texture	Grainy with contrasts in textural density, we've chosen speckled finishes and fine weaves with a little metallic lustre here and there.
Colour	Blending of many hues of pink, through to soft red, creates a soft, pleasing colour palette of muted, collaborative colours and tones.
Scale, proportion & balance	White sea salt and pink Himalayan salt make up most of the blend, with black pepper representing just 25 per cent – it is sprinkled through, as the eye is drawn to black and it becomes the peripheral element.
Rhythm & movement	Gritty yet softly integrating. There is an amalgamation as the individual elements merge.
Core feeling	HARMONY

Mood board

- crisp, modern, edgy combination of elements
- speckled vinyl
- salt crystal lamp
- modern, Nordic-style furniture
- rosy copper elements
- terrazzo and stone tiles
- Tibetan wool rug in colours graded through shades of grey, cream, light salmon to deep rosy terracotta
- natural cottons and linens in cool greys, creams and apricot
- paint colours in similar tones

Kieffer
PORTER'S PAINTS

DESIGNED SPACE

The glassed-in corner of this living room really sets the tone for this space. It's a straightforward room, stylishly put together with a colour palette of grey, pink and white, with the tiniest hint of black in the metal of the window frames. Although the colour palette is pastel, it is not at all sugary. The tones are subdued and mature, leaning more towards savoury than sweet.

The personality of the room is fresh and sophisticated. We used homeware retailer Occa-Home's Urban look, a blend of Scandi influences with contemporary furnishings and finishes with a minimalist edge. I like the contrast between the utilitarian grey vinyl flooring and the rug decorated with botanicals. Contemporary shapes are combined with smooth, tactile engineered finishes. A subtle shimmer from the rose gold and coppery lampshades elevates the atmosphere with that touch of luxe, as does the edgy, photocopied affordable art spontaneously stuck onto the walls with tape.

This interior includes all the classic elements, but almost everything has been given a contemporary twist.

FOLIAGE

Drawing inspiration from the verdant beauty of nature's bounty, I'm often even more inspired by foliage than I am by flowers. The different habits, shapes and shades of colour are astounding. Here we've only picked leaves of different shades of green – some are matt, others glossy, strappy, lacy, spiky, feathery; an abundance!

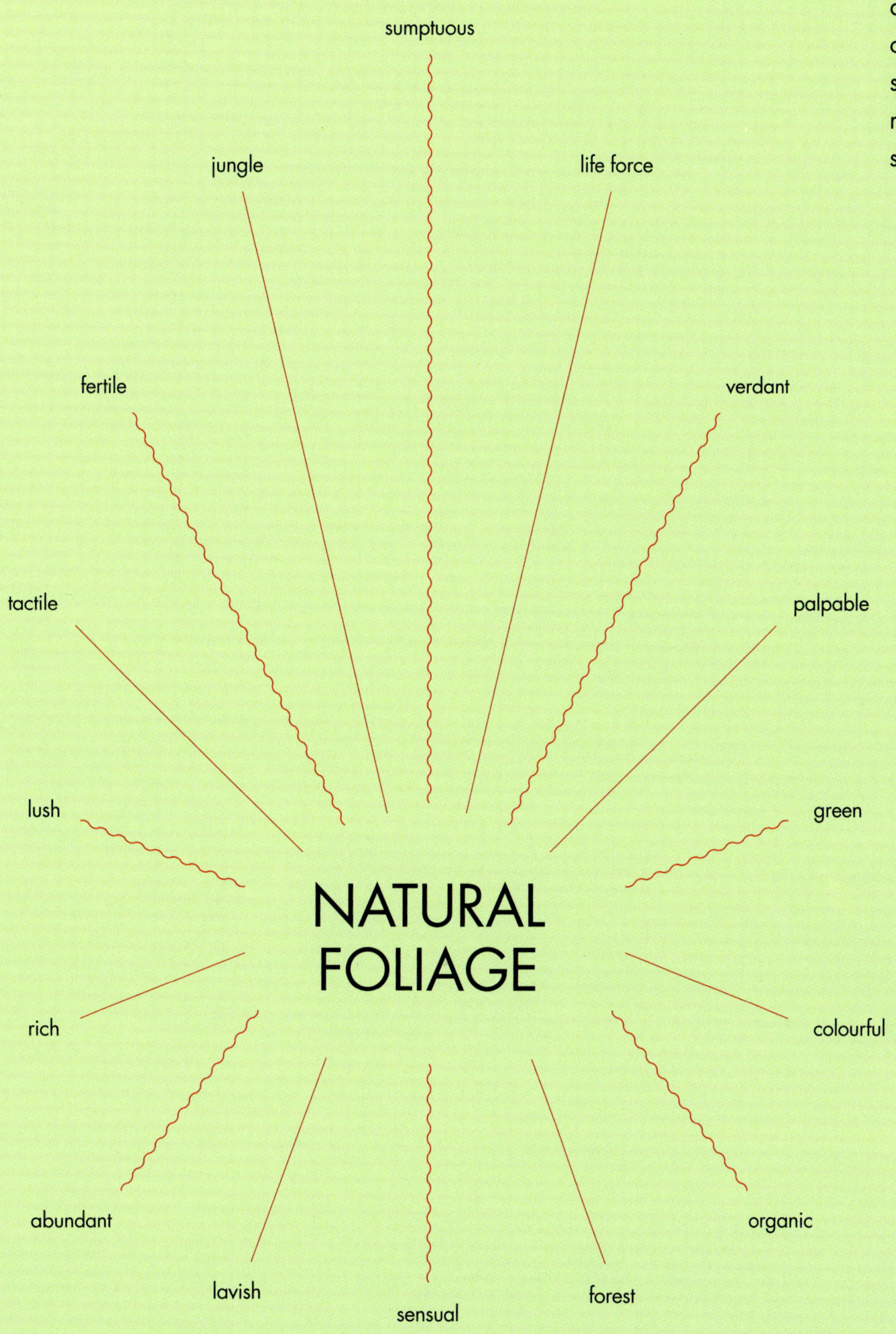

LET'S BREAK IT DOWN

Shape	A variety of shapes quite different from each other on the micro-level but that transform into something holistic and connected at a macro-level – from architectural and sculptural to curvy and organic. You could home in on one or work with a collection.
Line	Changing terrain that flows from one type to another. Combine different lines to create an assortment of shapes.
Texture	From smooth, glossy, fine variations through to coarse and spiky. There should be a rich mix of textures at play.
Colour	Earthy green, lime, khaki, avocado, jade, olive, emerald, bottle, sea, sage, mint, pea, golds, ambers, browns.
Scale, proportion & balance	Use different shades of green and a combination of various textures to create the visual weight within the interior composition.
Rhythm & movement	This inspiration calls for patterns and textures that break up the space and create interest along the way. Variety is key.
Core feeling	LUSH

Mood board

- a palette of materials in different textures and shades of green
- opulent brocade sari fabrics and other embroidered silks
- paintings by Marcella Kaspar of full-blown roses
- green translucent glass
- zinc paint finish for the walls
- we often have more than one choice for a key item on a mood board. Here, for example, there are three rug options: the peony Tibetan rug, the Terra Verde ombre-shaded rug and a deep green hemp rug

DESIGNED SPACE

This luscious interior is the work of artist Marcella Kaspar and builder/designer Mark Cooper. Yes, that is one of Marcella's glorious artworks on the wall. Right there, you have one of the room's strongest elements, which connects you immediately to the foliage inspiration.

Every element of this room showcases the verdant inspiration that is its design foundation: the various shades of green, the contrasting textures from powdery, grey-green lime-washed walls and charcoal granite floors through to the weather-worn timber of the coffee table, the linen on the sofa, the silk brocade cushions, the parchment lampshade, shiny, translucent green and amber glass and the sumptuous olive green rug with contrasting fibres of wool and gleaming silk.

PEBBLE
ROCK
STONE
TWIG

The energetic contrast of rounded, smooth pebble to jagged and angular rock, stone and spiky twigs are all at play here. Earth-centred, deep and fecund, these elements lure forth a moody, fertile and rich imagery, womb-like and comforting.

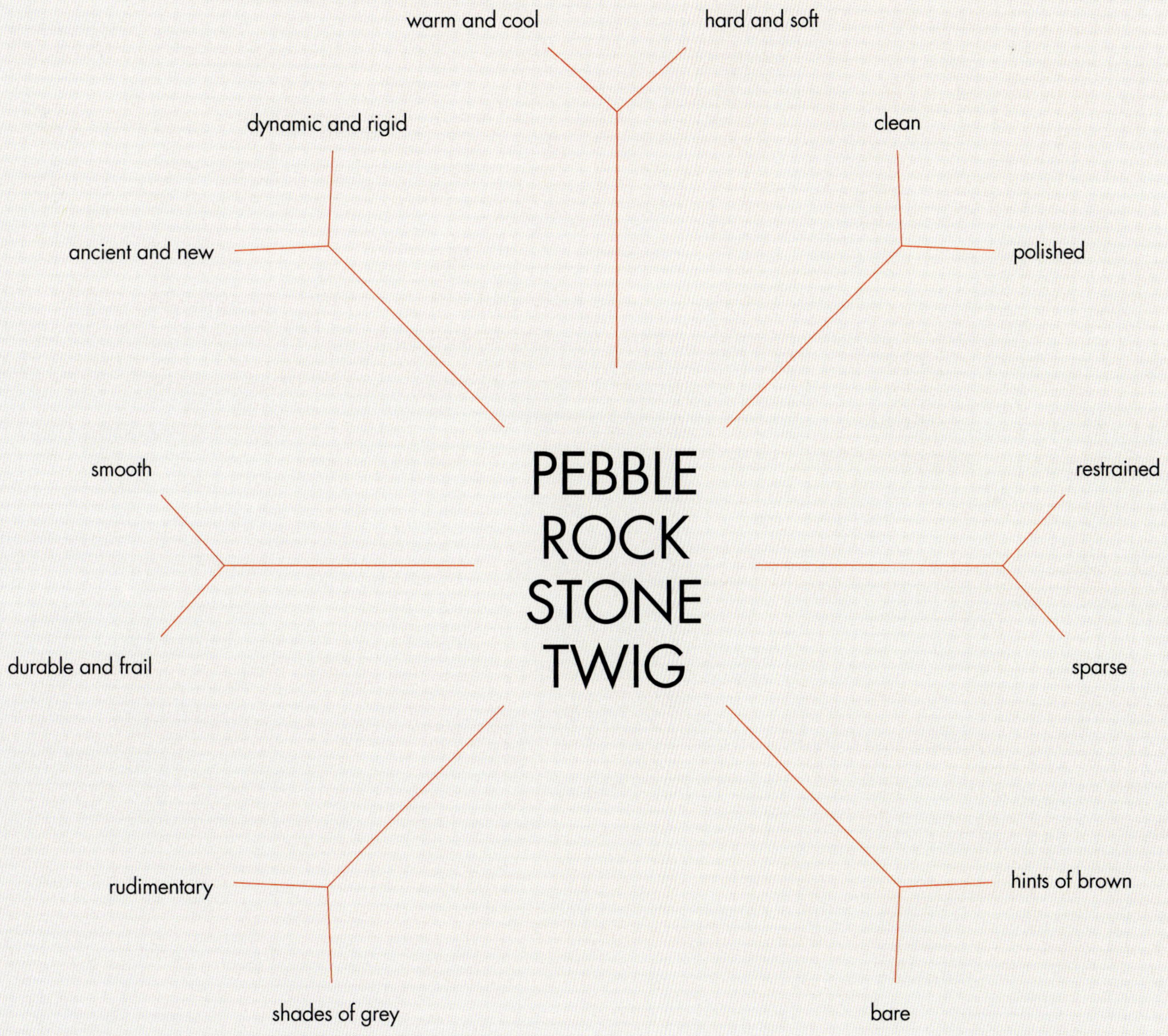

LET'S BREAK IT DOWN

Shape	Solid, rounded shapes and thin, angular – even awkward – lines side by side. Shapes don't have to match up to look good. Mismatching can work; I actually prefer it.
Line	Curved, vertical and angular lines work together. Vertical lines add height, horizontal lines add width, and angular ones keep things casual. Combinations need to be balanced to bring about equilibrium.
Texture	A combination of smooth and rough, refined yet rugged – all very tactile. Without this type of contrast in texture, the scheme could be boring and flat.
Colour	Light, mid and dark tones of grey, brown and white accents. You can play with a limited palette and still achieve maximum impact in your décor.
Scale, proportion & balance	Heavy and light – an asymmetrical balancing act. You can prevent design boredom with clever combinations.
Rhythm & movement	Relaxed – there is a progression through the gradation of colour. To keep a room alive, movement can be created through playing with sleek and shiny surfaces, contrasting with dull, matt and rough.
Core feeling	MOODY

Mood board

- a sumptuous, deep, dark and moody collection of elements
- lush velours
- felts
- woollen knits
- crispy linens
- glossy timber boards painted pale grey
- shaded carpets
- driftwood timber tiles
- nutty, woody elements in the furniture
- sculptural images of botanicals
- melancholy quirky artworks such as Paul Ryan's *Ping Pong Landscape*
- mid-century modern timber furniture in deep honey tones is a perfect partner for the rich layers of grey

DESIGNED SPACE

This tiny apartment in Cape Town shows restraint, while at the same time baring its sparse soul. It is both warm and cool. The warmth comes from the timber accents, the sheepskin thrown on the chair, the velvet-covered sofa and cushions and the timber floorboards. The shades-of-grey colour palette introduces a cool change. I love the different textures and moods of the greys: high gloss on the floor, matt on the walls, soft, lustrous fabrics on the lounge.

The furnishings are minimal. The chunky line of the L-shaped sofa contrasts with the angular, almost spindly, wooden armchair and coffee table. The differing visual weights of these pieces create an asymmetrical balance that generates a sense of equilibrium. The naïve way in which the humble artworks are grouped together and float, suspended in the middle of the wall, adds to the monastic, rudimentary feel of this interior.

LA VOCE
DELLE
PAROLES
OF IMAGES
ALBERGO
S. LUCIA

BOWL OF CHERRIES

Polished and elegant, the simplicity of this bowl of cherries invokes a sense of refined, rich, opulence that is graceful and sophisticated. The rich depth comes from the burnished brass bowl, the deep shades of glossy cherry red and elegant, haughty stems punching up into the air.

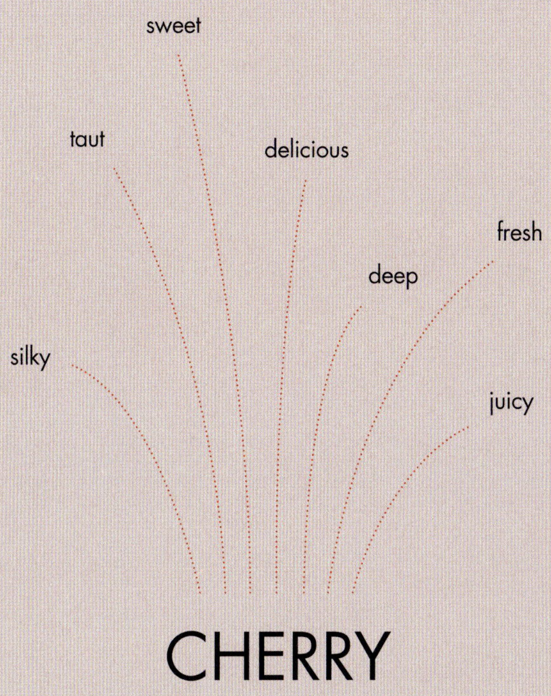

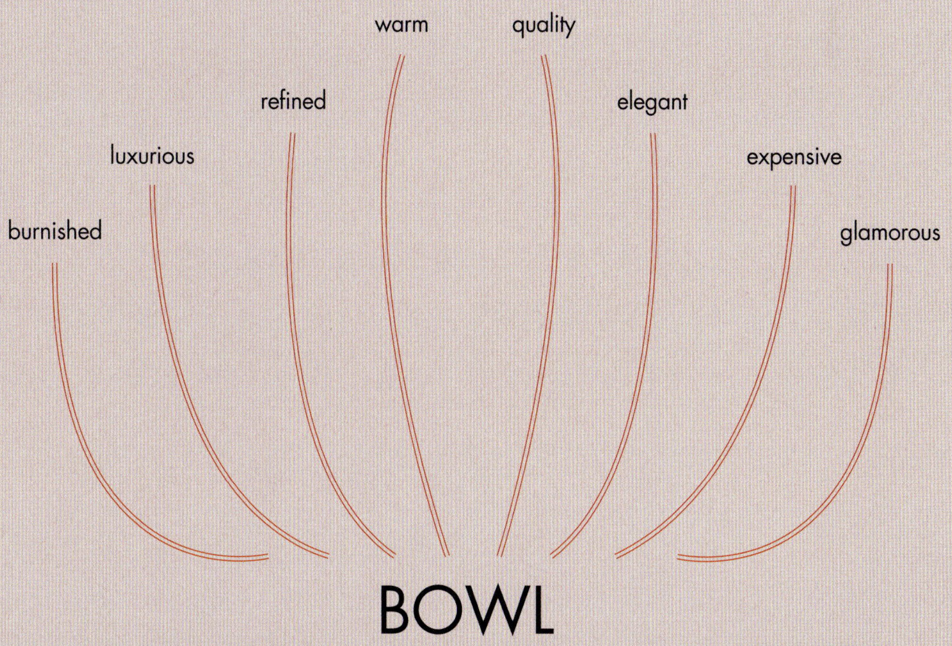

LET'S BREAK IT DOWN

Shape	Rounded, plump and full, with slender, elongated and elegant stems. Curvy shapes are appropriate, so too is an element of the sculptural.
Line	Curved and linear, yet mainly horizontal. Repetitious vertical lines can help create an assertive mood.
Texture	Polished, smooth and taut. Highly refined, lustrous and sophisticated with a psychological effect of being very dignified. Sleek, shiny surfaces reflect the light and draw attention to elements in the scheme.
Colour	Deep burgundy, clotted cream, burnished brass with a hint of charcoal. A balance of dark and light colours and reflective surfaces help create a warm room.
Scale, proportion & balance	Bottom-heavy large scale pieces of furniture balance out the grand proportions of the high-ceilinged room.
Rhythm & movement	Through repetition of object, line and colour you can create balance and a self-confident calm in the rhythm and movement within a space.
Core feeling	GLAMOROUS

Mood board

- pale stone
- large tiles
- decorative plaster mouldings
- brass light fittings inspired by mid-century modern
- elegant dining table with upholstered chairs
- upholstery options include leathers in cream and deep red, plain and quilted, as well as horsehair and plush wovens
- the glistening crystal drops suggest a chandelier for drama and theatre

handmade by
PORTER'S ORIGINAL PAINTS
Botticelli Angel
HOLLYWOODLAND
handmade by
PORTER'S ORIGINAL PAINTS
Chalk NSW
handmade by
PORTER'S ORIGINAL PAINTS

DESIGNED SPACE

Drawing upon mid-century modern Hollywood-style glamour, this elegant, generously proportioned dining room designed by Staffan Tollgård Design Group in London declares luxury and good taste. When I look at the image of this room it feels to me like a smart vintage tuxedo, with a black satin stripe down the side seam of the trousers, a wide-lapelled, cream jacket and a silk, burgundy bow tie. The repetitious vertical padding of the cream upholstery on the extra-long bespoke ivory leather banquette sets the tempo and rhythm of the interior scheme.

The squat, plump, cherry-red leather Maxalto Eunice dining chairs by Antonio Citterio at B&B Italia on the opposite side of the 1950s dining table are great equalisers in the linear space. The table's burnished bronze pedestal is the perfect match for the dashing light fittings on the wall. A smart combination of contrasting materials and textures and a wonderful mix of curvaceous and elongated shapes define this captivating interior. The abstract painting and crystal chandelier contribute to the theatrical feel of the décor and enhance the room's air of decadent elegance.

FLOWERS

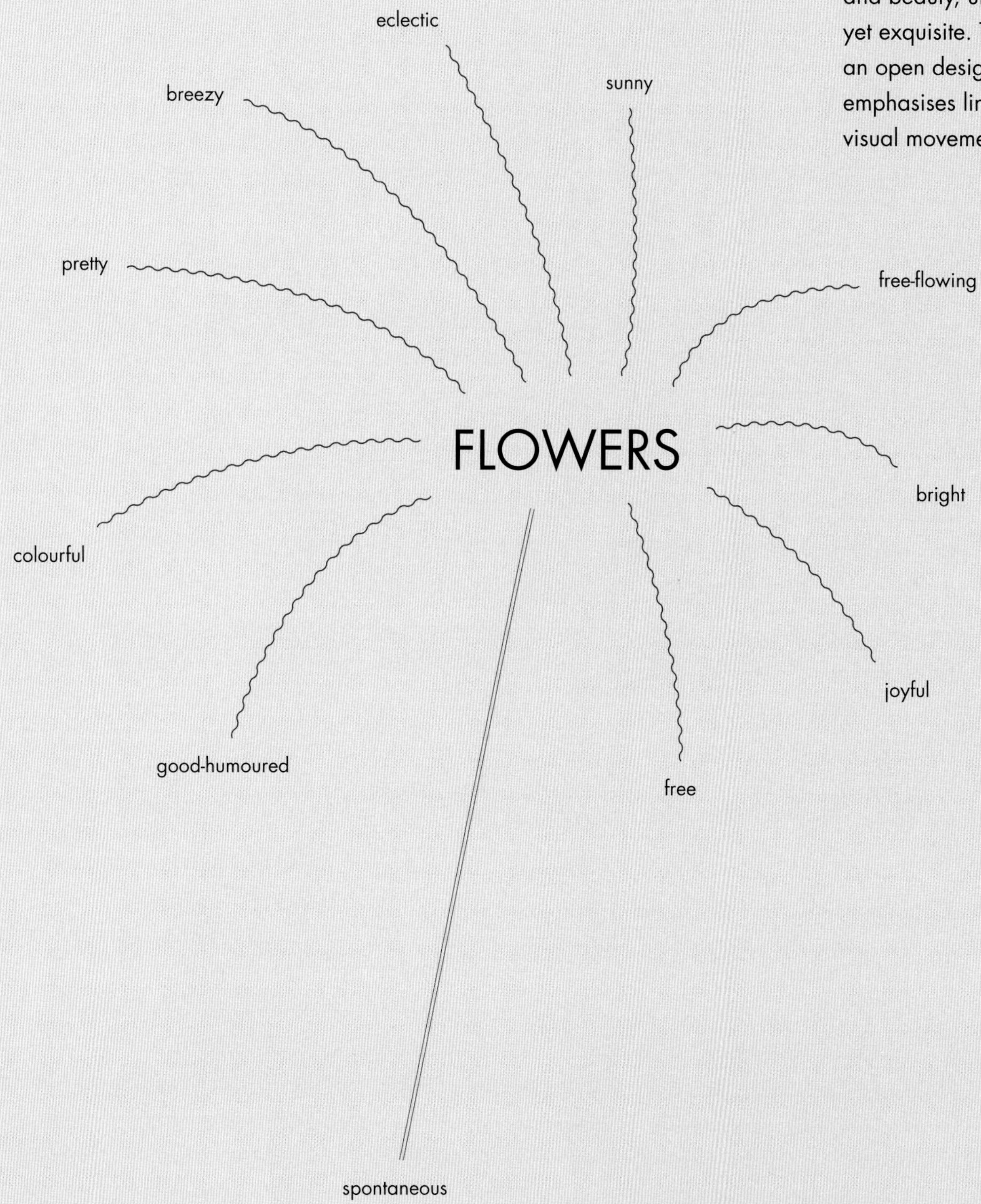

⬡ Fresh, floral bouquet in soft pretty colours with a mix of powdery foliage has a spontaneous feel, full of movement and with a free, unstructured and instinctive vibe. Flowers represent life and beauty, unpretentious, yet exquisite. They call for an open design style that emphasises line and visual movement.

LET'S BREAK IT DOWN

Shape	Contained, individual, free-form shapes that are varied and organic. This is another one that is all about the interesting mix of shapes.
Line	Creative line arrangement that has no set pattern and may have more than one focal point. It should be a mix of horizontal, vertical, oblique or zigzag – whichever way, it will be bold and dramatic.
Texture	Soft, feathery and delicate contrasted with rough, but leaning more to the delicate. It's very important to have at least one major rough textured element for the scheme to work well and give it depth.
Colour	Bright, clear pink and yellow, eucalyptus and silvery grey/greens, dusky blues and white. Don't be afraid of contrasting colours; look to Mother Nature for guidance. Matching colours dates an interior scheme.
Scale, proportion & balance	The grouping of the flowers in a bunch creates a kind of harmony, a mixture of radial and asymmetrical. You need a bit of a break in symmetry so things don't look too boring and contrived.
Rhythm & movement	Upbeat, varied, stimulating and full of life force. Through transition, progression, contrast and repetition you can create a lively rhythm and movement to a space.
Core feeling	HAPPY

Mood board

- a pretty scheme with shades of blue and accents of hot pink and bright, sunny yellow
- furniture and lighting are an eclectic mix of vintage and reproduction styles
- an over-dyed, vintage-style rug anchors the look

Modern
PORTER'S
ORIGINAL
PAINTS
PORTER'S
ORIGINAL
PAINTS

DESIGNED SPACE

This interior is so much like its inspiration. There are wonderful jolts of colour throughout and the eclectic mix is reminiscent of a posy of effortlessly mismatched flowers, picked on a walk in the countryside, which together look extraordinary.

The mad mix-and-match of furnishing styles, from mid-century modern to Victorian, looks spontaneous and fun. There are some wonderful examples of lighting from the mid-century modern era. The hot pink fabric upholstery on the antique sofa makes the whole scheme feel more contemporary. The pale blue-grey walls and white-painted timber floors are anchored by a distressed black rug that is brand new yet looks virtually threadbare, suggesting the march of time.

The furniture is arranged so that it seems to radiate out from the coffee table. This tight grouping loosens as you move further through the room, just like – yes, you guessed it – an opening flower.

BRINGING THE OUTDOORS IN

THE NATURAL OPTIONS

What we are saying is: don't be limited to an 'interior' way of thinking. Looking at your indoors with an *outdoor* vision can create a lot of life force. Placing plants indoors is the simplest way to create the atmosphere of an interior garden, but there are many other options as well.

Let's look at the many ways that nature has found its way into our homes and how the natural world has played its part in influencing furniture and homeware design.

Here are the first twenty ideas, off the top of my head:

- Recycled timber vaulted ceilings
- Slate bathrooms
- Gabion stone walls
- Leather floors
- Copper bathtubs
- Clay pottery plates and mugs
- Linen sheets
- Bamboo-handled cutlery
- Rain chains in indoor courtyards
- Vertical garden walls
- Silk or cashmere rugs
- Rammed-earth walls
- Trees inside, growing through cut-outs in the floor
- Conservatory rooms
- Walls clad in black bamboo
- Large ceiling window right above the bed
- EcoSmart ethanol fires
- Beeswax candles everywhere
- Cork furniture
- Handmade woollen felt blankets

Use natural materials

Choosing natural, organic materials for your walls, floors, ceilings, furniture, soft furnishings and bedding is one of the easiest ways to bring the outdoors in. The extent to which you go with this will depend on your own personal style.

Some people love rugged, raunchy, bare stone walls, while others prefer to introduce nature in a different way – for example, by choosing a granular sand paint, a matt paint with real sand grains in it, to give their walls a subtle texture. Porter's Paints are the masters of this technique, using very fine granules of lime in the paint to give an ultra-matt finish. Their lime wash paints are to die for; they cover up a multitude of sins and turn a boring wall into sheer luxury . . . trust me!

Some people love recycled, gnarly, old timber floorboards made from planks rescued from an old wharf or railway yard, while others would rather have polished timber parquetry floors in an elegant herringbone design. The volume can be turned up or down, depending on your personal taste – it is up to you to work out the balance that suits best.

Use motifs from nature

Flora and fauna have been used throughout the ages as decorative motifs on homeware such as fabrics, tiles, wallpapers, crockery and glassware. Some motifs become fashionable for one reason or another; there is always an ebb and flow to the cycle of what may be popular at a given time. The one constant is that the archives we draw upon belong to Mother Nature.

Flowers, birds, bees and other nature motifs appear on everything from fabrics, wallpaper, cushions and bedlinen through to plates and drinking glasses. From time to time, even the humble pineapple provides inspiration for decorative items.

Use the elements

Air

Not everyone has the luxury of floor-to-ceiling glazed thresholds such as sliding glass doors to separate the indoors and outdoors but there are many other ways to bring that airy, breezy feel to an interior space. You could include elements that move with the air, such as sheer fabric drops, mobiles, and garlands. You could also have scented flowers and indoor plants and burn essential oils to scent and purify the air. Banksia pod diffusers, with essential oils from your favourite plants, introduce an even more natural ingredient to the home.

Decorating with whites, creams and light colours will also evoke that 'lightness of air' feeling. In warmer climates ceiling fans are instantly calming. In cool climates, burning sage or incense will relax you and give you a sense of warmth and wellbeing.

Water

Using water features indoors engenders a sense of coolness and calm. In hot, dry climates indoor water features are practical as well, because as air currents pass over or through the wet surface they provide passive, evaporative cooling.

If you love the sound of trickling water, you could have an indoor fountain, though I am just as happy to hear water outside, the sound drifting in when the doors and windows are open. I really love the idea of crossing a threshold of water when entering the interior space by having a shallow pool of water with paved steps across it, or having an interior courtyard Geoffrey Bawa-style with a still, reflective body of water within it. That is a blissful thing to live with every day. I am showing my Sri Lankan heritage here!

If you don't have enough space for a water feature, you can do what people do all over Sri Lanka, in temples and homes, from the most luxurious to the most humble – fill a simple bowl with water, then place a layer of floating flowers on top. You could use one type of flower or a mixture, or you could create a mandala-style design. Bowls of flowers are often placed in entrances in Sri Lanka as a beautiful, tranquil welcome statement. They also work well as the centrepiece on a table or as small, individual place-setters for a dinner party.

One of the most amazing uses of water indoors that I've seen recently was by the talented innovator, Japanese floral artist Azuma Makoto. He suspended living flowers and foliage in huge blocks of ice that were about a metre tall, 60 cm wide and 38 cm deep. After the blocks were formed in an industrial-size ice-cube tray, Makoto shaped them with a bandsaw so that he could control the final composition of each one. Since Makoto's *Iced Flowers* exhibit, many florists have started freezing blooms in ice to use as table top decorations for parties and other events.

Fire

If I've had a really stressful day at work, I don't turn on any electric lighting when I get home. I have candlelight only and I can't describe how calming and soothing this is. I'm sure most of you have experienced at least a bath by candlelight, so you can imagine the blissful effect. Grouping lit candles together creates a wonderful effect, as does a candelabra, whether standing, pendant or tabletop.

You don't need a fireplace to have a fire indoors. You can buy ethanol fires in every size for interiors – you can even get one that sits on a tabletop. Plus, they are portable, so can be moved around the house. Some ethanol burners don't provide heating but merely a decorative flame, like a big candle, to create that feeling of gathering around a campfire. Placing your candles and burners on mirrored surfaces will amplify the effect.

Earth

If you have the space, the best way to introduce the element of earth into your home is with an interior garden. In my house in Avalon I've made two openings in the floor of my living room in which I've planted *Ficus lyrata* (fiddle-leaf fig trees) and underplanted them with anthurium, *Philodendron xanadu* and ferns. These openings are on the western side of the house where there is floor-to-ceiling glazing and therefore maximum light.

You could also make a zen garden with gravel and rocks and some air plants, which grow without soil. Rocks, pebbles and crystals make beautiful, earthy indoor decorations, too. For a different take on such things, I love the Himalayan salt lamps and selenite crystal lamps that create a beautiful ambient glow and are said to help with the natural ionisation of the air.

Sunlight and shade

A simple but powerful way to bring the outdoors in is to introduce some sunlight – it brings life to any room, making colours zing, and adding a healthy feeling to the space. The more windows, doorways, internal light wells and skylights you have, the better.

Another trick is to 'paint' with light by controlling the way it casts shadows onto various surfaces – remembering that textured surfaces absorb light and glossy surfaces reflect it. You may also choose to colour the light as it flows through the glass. Frank Lloyd Wright was a master at this, designing thousands of geometric stained-glass panels.

Indirect lighting works well too. There are many ways to create amazing, tranquil dapple effects to emulate the natural dappling outside. You could position trees and other plants close to the house, or use fabrics, screens, blinds and perforated panelling (slim panels of timber or metal with symmetrically placed holes drilled into them) to direct sunlight through onto interior surfaces. Use whatever you can think of to filter direct daylight and allow for shadow play.

Shade is almost as important as light – you don't want to flood a space with too much light because this can ruin the ambience. A clever use of shade can really show off the architecture.

On this page you can see an art piece I made with slices of doors from houses damaged in Hurricane Katrina. The salvage yard I found them in puts all the proceeds from the sales of building remnants from the hurricane into rebuilding New Orleans, which is a real testament to the fighting spirit of the community.

Indoor plants

Indoor plants not only make our interior spaces more beautiful and stylish but also purify the air, improve productivity and reduce stress levels. Put simply, plants make people feel good.

Structured, architectural plants are a favourite of mine as they are like living sculptures. There are so many types of foliage to choose from – you are bound to find a shape, texture, habit and colour to suit your taste.

When you are selecting your indoor plants, key things to think about are how much sunlight your space receives and how much time and TLC you can give your plants. We are all juggling busy lives so we want maximum effect for the least amount of effort. In other words – low-maintenance plants.

HERE ARE SOME OF OUR FAVOURITE INDOOR PLANTS

Codiaeum variegatum spp. **(Rushfoil, croton)**

A must-have in any indoor garden. Its foliage is a standout, with tropical waxy variegated and often colourful leaves.

Adiantum aethiopicum **(Maidenhair fern)**

Its fine, lacy foliage has a beautiful ethereal quality and it is the most lush green colour with dark (almost black) thin stems.

Ficus elastica **(Burgundy or rubber plant)**

This handsome house plant has dark burgundy-green leathery leaves. You will need to wipe its leaves free of dust from time to time.

Clivia miniata **(Clivia)**

An elegant strappy evergreen with stunning orange trumpet flowers. This is a shade-loving plant so will do well indoors, with some filtered light.

Canna spp. **(Canna lily)**

This lovely fern has blue/grey-green, almost silvery foliage with reddish-purple stalks that are really good for brightening dark spots in the garden.

Bromeliad **(Bromeliad)**

These come in a wide variety of types, sizes, shapes and foliage colours. The one shown here is Guzmania, which has bright green foliage with colourful flower spikes that can last many months.

Sansevieria trifasciata laurentii **(Snake plant)**

Sometimes referred to as mother-in-law's tongue, this is a robust succulent with dramatic upright foliage. Great in low light.

Zamioculcas zamiifolia **(ZZ plant)**

This beautiful bullet-proof plant has gorgeous dark-green glossy leaves and grows well indoors.

Asplenium nidus 'Norfolk Gem' **(Bird's nest fern)**

This has lovely large fronds, similar to a banana leaf, and makes a very attractive indoor plant.

Strelitzia reginae **(Bird of paradise)**

The flower does look like the head of an exotic bird. The most common type has orange flowers, but newer varieties have yellow and blue flowers.

Monstera deliciosa **(Fruit salad plant)**

Also known as the Swiss cheese plant because of the holes in its leathery, glossy leaves. It's a dramatic old favourite.

Dracaena marginata **(Dragon tree)**

An attractive, spiky-leaved plant with colourful foliage. This a strong, low-maintenance, drought-tolerant plant.

Calathea spp. **(Peacock plant)**

This plant has striking, ornately striped foliage that almost look like it has been painted. This plant is not grown for its flowers, it's all about the foliage!

Licuala ramsayi spp. **(Australian fan palm)**

This is one of the most majestic palms with its jagged windmill-like leaves. It's great indoors; keep it well watered in warmer months.

Anthurium spp. **(Laceleaf)**

This tropical plant, with dark heart-shaped glossy green leaves and unusual flowers, is the perfect house plant.

Phalaenopsis spp. **(Phalaenopsis orchid)**

This is one of the easiest types of orchid to grow. Don't discard it when it stops flowering. With proper care, blooms will return.

Doodia aspera **(Prickly rasp fern)**

This Australian native makes an excellent indoor plant, and adapts well to both shady and sunny areas. New growth fronds are bright pink.

Nephrolepis exaltata 'Bostoniensis' **(Boston fern)**

A very easy fern to grow indoors. Rotate the pot from time to time to ensure symmetrical growth.

Dieffenbachia spp. **(Dumb cane)**

Beautiful mix of green/white/yellow variegated foliage. Looks fantastic and is a beauty for indoor planting.

Howea forsteriana **(Kentia palm)**

A great Australian native palm with a lean trunk and drooping crown of dark green fronds. It can be grown almost anywhere as an indoor plant.

Cissus antarctica **(Kangaroo vine)**

Hardy with fuzzy foliage, it's also a creeper, so is great for verticality. New growth has a coppery hue that changes to a rainforest green.

Schefflera actinophylla **(Umbrella plant)**

An evergreen with amazing radiating foliage, but no flowers. Grown indoors, it can be kept to a manageable size.

Senecio rowleyanus **(String of pearls)**

This perennial vine is a favourite of mine. It's not fussy as long as it gets bright light and is kept a little dry. Its beaded tendrils are striking.

Pachypodium lamerei **(Madagascar palm)**

It's not a palm at all, but a member of the succulent family. As long as you can give it lots of direct sunlight, it will thrive indoors.

HOUSE PLANT HEALTH

To check whether there is enough light in the chosen spot, do a shadow test. Hold your hand against a piece of white paper; if your hand casts a shadow you have enough light for most house plants.

Feed your house plants with slow-release fertiliser granules tucked under the mulch and remember to remove dust from the leaves regularly.

Water house plants only when they need it. Most problems are due to over-watering. Just do the fingertip test to check whether soil is dry. If in doubt, it's better not to water. You can also water using a spray bottle.

All house plants should regularly spend some time outdoors if possible to stay healthy, but don't leave them out in the direct sun or they may burn.

Rotate your plants by a half-turn every two weeks to give them all equal exposure to the light.

Hanging plants

Thank goodness there is finally another option for hanging plants other than the dreary wire baskets lined with coconut fibre that our nanas had on their verandahs! Bless.

Hanging pot plants fill up superfluous space in the home, and planters are available in a variety of decorative shapes, materials and colours – everything from plants wrapped in moss and fluoro string, upside-down pots, jelly mould shapes, ceramic vessels in stunning glazes and patterns to my personal favourites, macramé single, double and triple tier pot-holders that come in natural twines as well as jewel-coloured rope. Some air plants or epiphytes (right) don't even need to be contained, they can be freely suspended anywhere.

For most of us living in the city, where every centimetre matters, hanging plants allow you to fill your home with beautiful, oxygen-giving living things, and also to maximise visual impact without losing precious living space.

PLANTER POINTS

Make sure that whatever you hang your planter from can support the weight of pot, plant and soil. Remember that wet soil can be heavy when you add it to the weight of the plant plus the pot. Choose a lightweight potting soil mix.

Don't fill your pot right up to the edge with soil because when you water, your loose soil is likely to drip over the edge of the pot. Make sure the soil is a couple of centimetres below the top lip of the pot.

If you've planted straight into the pot, check that it has drainage holes and either attach a saucer to the bottom or take the plants down when you water them to protect your floors. Or, to solve this problem, just place your pot plant into the hanging planter without planting directly into it.

Staghorns and elkhorns

I love staghorn and elkhorn ferns; they look amazing indoors. These nostalgic plants conjure fond memories of parents and grandparents. I really like them for their prehistoric feel and banana-peel-eating ways.

They are an ideal way to add greenery to any space, and make an interesting, unique feature grouped together and hung on a wall by themselves or with paintings and other wall art.

Platycerium superbum and *Platycerium grande*, commonly known as the staghorn fern, and the closely related *Platycerium bifurcatum*, known as the elkhorn fern, are epiphytic ferns, meaning they grow, without soil, on the trunk or branches of trees or on fallen logs, and sometimes even on rocks. They are native to tropical and temperate areas of Australia, such as rainforests, and are available from nurseries, normally mounted onto a backing board of some sort. You can either hang them individually or you could attach two boards back-to-back so you have a plant on both sides. These spectacular plants will grow just about anywhere in filtered light.

Why not create a staghorn and elkhorn chandelier by suspending smaller, baby ferns in an uneven cluster from the ceiling? Or you could just hang one larger, well-established one.

YOTAM OTTOLENGHI
PLENTY MORE
CHINCHIN
FLAVOURS OF MELBOURNE

LOOKING AFTER STAGS

Feed staghorns and elkhorns your banana peels, as they make a great DIY fertiliser. Apart from other benefits, bananas contain potassium, which helps displace sodium that could be harmful to salt-sensitive staghorns.

The smaller elkhorn has multiple babies or rosettes (spores or pups) of foliage which can be easily separated and propagated to form new plants.

Elks and stags produce two types of fronds, fertile and sterile. Fertile fronds have brown, rusty-coloured tips underneath, where they produce their spores. That is the sign of a healthy adult plant. The dead (sterile) fronds attach the plant to its support and gather the fallen leaves, creating their own compost for roots, moisture and nutrients. Isn't nature amazing?!

Keep stags and elks slightly dry in colder months. Both grow well outdoors as far south as Melbourne, but regular frosts will harm them.

If well established, they will tolerate periods of drought, but in dry weather a good soaking once a week will help, especially when you are trying to establish younger plants or ones that have been moved.

Indoor miniature gardens

Another way to introduce plants inside is to create miniature gardens inside your home. No matter what the size of the space you live in you can always find a way to create a garden. Here are a few ideas.

Bonsai

Bonsai is an ancient form of gardening. The word 'bonsai' in Japanese means 'plantings in tray'. Bonsai uses cultivation techniques such as pruning, root reduction, potting, defoliation and grafting to produce small trees that mimic the shape and style of mature, full-size trees. Although bonsai are often planted on their own, you can also create a bonsai forest (or group planting) mimicking trees in nature.

Bonsai is a beautiful art form for people who love the nurturing and aesthetic aspects of gardening but have limited space.

It can be a bit tricky to grow bonsai indoors, but some species can tolerate indoor conditions and thrive with the correct placement and care. As with all plants, first you need to consider the needs of each individual plant in terms of light, water and temperature. You should also make sure that you give your bonsai regular time outdoors for it to really thrive. One idea is to have a couple or more bonsai that you rotate, so that half stay outside and the other half indoors, and then swap them around at regular intervals. This way you will keep them in tip-top condition.

Terrariums

Terrariums are a perfect way to bring a touch of nature indoors; no wonder everyone loves them.

There are two types – open and closed. Open terrariums are for plants that can tolerate direct sunlight, and closed ones for those that need a lot of moisture and can tolerate indirect light but don't put them in direct light as the heat could cook them.

When choosing a container make sure it is made of glass or another clear material that light can pass through, as all plants need light to grow. Select your plants carefully, because they should all have similar moisture and light requirements. For example, you might select a group of drought-tolerant plants or shade-loving plants to live together.

We've chosen shade-loving types such as: *Begonia rex*, *Syngonium* (green/white) *Fittonia* (pink and green/crème), and baby's tears. Have fun!

TERRARIUM WORKSHOP

Open terrariums should be kept moist, but you have to be careful not to over-water them. Closed terrariums need little or no water. Succulent and cactus terrariums are more bullet-proof and need less maintenance than other plant types.

Select all the items you need: all-purpose potting mix, gravel, charcoal pellets, moss, plants, glass container, variety of pebbles/stones, décor items.

Place 2.5 cm of gravel at the bottom of the container. The total depth of your gravel, charcoal, moss and soil should equal about one-third of the height of the container.

Sprinkle a thin layer of charcoal pellets over the gravel. Charcoal helps keep soil fresh and is available online or from pet stores.

Add a layer of sheet moss, which you can buy off the shelf at most nurseries or order by the bag from most florists.

Place a layer of soil over the moss. The soil type will depend on the plants you've chosen. We used all-purpose potting mix for our shade-loving plants.

Nestle plants into the soil, up to the moss layer, building up soil around the base of each. We broke begonia and baby's tears up into smaller plantings.

Add some larger rocks and pebbles in different areas to create your mini-terrain.

Decorate with small animal figures, seashells or anything your heart desires.

Finally, give your terrarium a good drink of water using a spray bottle, which gives you more control as you can direct where the water goes.

Some other ideas

Found objects

Objet d'art, literally 'art object' or 'work of art' in French, has become quite a flexible term, used to describe everything outside the major categories of serious art you might use to decorate your home. It can include such things as feathers, stones, shells, fossils, twigs, branches, pebbles and seed pods.

You can display found objects from nature and repurpose them as works of art. As pristine nature is disappearing or being compromised around the world, natural objects are becoming more revered.

There are many ways to display your found objects to great effect – you don't have to worry about rules. You might like to group a selection of items together on a tray, shelf or tabletop to create artistic still-life vignettes around your home. You can mix the colours up or keep to one colour palette, but mix the textures and finishes for accent.

I usually style vignettes using three or four elements, making sure that at least one or two of the items are real stand-out pieces. To create a cohesive composition, I like to vary the height and scale so they look good together. Repetition is another great way to create strong impact. Displaying the same objects in a linear, minimal way throughout a space can be very effective.

THE DESIGN BOOK

Flowers: dead or alive

I love the spontaneous, uncontrived look of floral arrangements. As with food, floral designers and growers around the world are moving towards seasonal, sustainable, locally grown flowers. There is a wonderful poetry to working in alignment with the rhythms of nature.

Bouquet arrangements that are loose, natural and authentic are the most appealing. Mix unusual colour combinations with interesting botanical specimens and seasonal foliage. I am especially fond of those bouquets that appear stitched up but have a renegade bloom or two that launches itself off to one side or the other, really evoking the feeling of spontaneity.

We try to acknowledge the beauty of flowers at every stage of their life; when they're fresh and pert, as they wilt and even once they're dead. Don't think you have to throw them out as soon as a few of them start to fall. Try to appreciate them in their faded glory; their delicacy and, at the same time, strength. Enjoy the impact their form and beauty have on you.

There are so many creative ways to display flowers – let your imagination run wild. One single bloom in a humble glass bottle can have just as much impact as a bouquet in an ornate vase. It all depends on the art of placement, by which I mean paying attention to the feeling of balance and harmony created by the way you orientate things in your environment.

Wabi sabi – the art of imperfection

Wabi sabi is not just a decorating style but rather a mind-set, originating from Zen-Buddhism. The essence of this philosophy is centred around the acceptance that all things in life are transient and imperfect. Everything around us is always in a state of flux, changing, ageing, breaking down and dying – yet there is beauty in every aspect of this journey. *Wabi sabi* is all about embracing these changes and appreciating all of it. I love this philosophy and am innately drawn to it.

Art

So much wonderful art, sculpture and photography celebrates our connection to nature and is another wonderful way to bring that realm into our homes. Many artists directly incorporate elements of nature into their artworks. Others create their own interpretations through their chosen medium, eloquently capturing the natural force. Some kind of magical transfer occurs, and you can feel the synergistic pull towards the subject matter that the artist must have also felt in creating it.

Lighting

You can create an outdoor feeling inside your home through the way you light it. Rather than using masses of overhead lighting to flood your home, think about creating more atmosphere, with areas of light and shade, through resort-style warm, concealed white lighting.

Party lights, traditionally used outdoors, can look very pretty indoors. So can paper lanterns, candles and hurricane lamps.

Become aware of how lighting feels and looks outside – it is hardly ever flat and consistent. Most often it is textured and playful, evoking different feeling and moods. Interior lighting can be the same. Different forms can create texture and layers in the light, so think about the moods you love to live with and try to create that same effect. Think of lighting as a textural tool to create atmosphere.

My favourite light is dappled sunlight as it passes through the leaves of a tree and covers the ground with a random pattern of circular or elliptical pools of light. It makes your heart sing. Essentially, that is the lesson of the artful implementation of lighting texture right there!

Outdoor furniture

There is something refreshing about mixing what is traditionally regarded as 'outdoor' furniture with indoor furnishings. Items such as canvas director's chairs, deckchairs, wicker armchairs or sofas, butterfly chairs, garden benches, wooden picnic or card tables, daybeds or even swings that usually hang from a tree branch can look amazing inside your home mixed with more refined, traditional 'indoor' pieces.

By using outdoor furniture and accessories indoors you can really make yourself feel as though your home is a relaxing, resort-style sanctuary. As the boundaries between outside and inside continue to blur, there are more and more transterior products coming onto the market that can sit comfortably in either space.

There are so many wonderful ways to bring the beauty and life force of nature into your home and I hope I've inspired you to do so in abundance. It really is a sign of the times that more and more of us are innately drawn to do this because we are missing the feeling of connection to the great outdoors. In our busy modern day-to-day lives in concrete urban jungles, we don't have the opportunity to be outdoors, in wilderness areas. Going for a jog on the beach, or walking the dog in the park is as close as it gets. So these tokens of nature that we live with and decorate our homes with become quite sacred and meaningful.

TEN ROOMS

WORKING WITH A BLANK CANVAS

Nadine and I decided that the best way to show you our interior design philosophy in action was to find a 'blank canvas' space and decorate it in different ways, as different rooms in a home. We decided to use two different sections of one large, empty open-plan industrial warehouse space. It's on street level and has concrete floors throughout and multiple sources of natural light. I'll call the different spaces Space A and Space B.

We have created five different room sets in Space A, and another five in Space B. Each of the ten rooms is totally different. It's amazing how changing materials, colours, textures and furnishings can achieve different results within the same shell. All of the paint colours we refer to are Porter's.

Please keep in mind that these were room 'sets' to illustrate how I would approach different outcomes within the same space, so we didn't install functional lighting but only decorative lighting (some of which is functional as well). Functional lighting provides the illumination you need to do your daily activities. It's the practical aspect of lighting, such as having good lighting in the bathroom when you're shaving or putting on your makeup, or overhead lighting at your kitchen counter for cooking at night. Decorative lighting is used to highlight different elements of interior design such as artworks, plants, a grouping of furniture or to create ambience.

SPACE

A

Space A is in a corner of the warehouse with a beautiful rustic, distressed brick wall and four large, original windows. The adjacent wall is plain and rendered, with a vertical concrete column.

SPLIT-LEVEL BEDROOM

Changing the levels in a space is one of my favourite things to do because it immediately changes the dynamic. In an open-plan situation, it is also a great way to designate different living zones. I believe that humans feel most comfortable in spaces that follow nature. It's not easy to replicate nature because it's just too good, however, just as topography of land changes, it's nice to sometimes reproduce that effect indoors as it really changes the perception and feel of the space.

Floors and walls

We covered the floors in Texas, a beautiful cork-effect vinyl tile, which gives the room a rich, textured, earthy base, almost like a forest floor. The concrete platform and solid timber step add a modern, industrial edge. The walls were painted in Watermark, a cloudy white to the left of the concrete column, and Overland, which looks like wet sand, on the right.

Furniture

The Big Bug armchair at the foot of the bed is by one of my favourite designers, Paola Navone. To my eye, it looks like a pebble-shaped daybed – it's so organic and smart. We mixed up the new and old with the antique chair covered in gold silk velvet and adorned with a sweet cushion heavily embroidered in flowers. It sits alongside the JD brass-caged occasional tables with Indian rosewood tops.

Plants

A young olive tree, jade plant, staghorn and elkhorn and trailing *Rhipsalis* help to bring nature inside.

Soft furnishings

Blooms are reimagined on luxurious silk satin and velvet cushions by Ellie Cashman combined with a hand-felted wool blanket by the talented Jacqui Fink, and pure linen sheets to evoke a sense of raw elegance on the bed.

Decoration

The black-and-white photographic print of a desert scene by Ross Lawrence is a contrast to the delectable, thick oil painting, *Blue Magenta*, by Alesandro Ljubicic, yet both bring nature into the room magnificently. You can see other traces of the outside in the vintage cement, outdoor pig statues, the coral skeleton on a stand and the Australian painted timber bowl.

Lighting
The Spillray, a cluster of Italian-made blown glass with a bronze metallic pendant light, is hung off-centre to create a moody, light-and-shade effect.

Accents
We used a coarse particleboard to create a rustic headboard for the bed, which also doubles as a shelf. The texture of the board is similar to a stack of hay bales and brings a wonderful sense of the outdoors into the room.

TRANSTERIOR ELEMENTS

1. Level changes to mimic natural land topography
2. Natural cork-effect tile to connect the floors to the bark of the cork tree
3. Concrete-coloured platform a typically exterior finish brought inside.
4. Plants help bring nature inside
5. Photograph of the desert
6. Pebble-shaped daybed
7. Cushions heavily embroidered in flowers
8. Oil painting, *Blue Magenta*, bringing floral imagery inside
9. Outdoor pig statues
10. Coral skeleton on a stand
11. The indigenous Australian painted timber bowl
12. Coarse particleboard used to create a rustic headboard for the bed

BATHROOM

I love this bathroom! It's the perfect combination of old with new, yet it still exudes a luxurious flavour, set off by rich colours and lush plantings. I designed the JD solid cedar wood bathtub and basin. I was inspired by my trips to Kyoto where solid wood Japanese soaking tubs are part of an ancient tradition. What I love most about them is that you really do feel wrapped up in nature when you bathe, and this feeling is amplified when they are brought inside. I've used the same tub in my own homes. We wanted to create a garden courtyard feeling within this room – dark, moody and lush. Visceral and sumptuously romantic too. The floating wall wrapped in sharkskin wallpaper breaks up the space and helps create a sense of intimacy and enclosure.

Floors and walls
We left the concrete floor as is and painted the walls with Maidenhair green matte acrylic paint. We then installed a vertical garden on the wall as a verdant backdrop to the bathtub. You could lie back and soak in the bath, gazing at the greenery, seeing the fern fronds swaying in the breeze through the open windows, enjoying the garden's earthy fragrance.

Furniture
Contemporary design pieces such as a modern matte black Cosmic Hiro timber stool, a towel stand, freestanding shelves and a self-supporting framed mirror are combined with a variety of outdoor items such as a distressed, vintage-green metal potting bench, used for storage, folding café chairs, rattan armchair and small café table; together they give this bathroom an alfresco air.

Soft furnishings
I love the cowhides on the floor and a reindeer pelt on the rattan chair as they bring a sense of raw luxury to the space.

Accents
The floating wall is dramatically wrapped in Porter's Zigrino wallpaper in a black sharkskin print.

Lighting
An antique chandelier converted to a tabletop version sits on the vintage bistro/café table next to the tub and the only other thing you need when in the bath, of course, are candles!

Plants
In the vertical garden there are Boston and maidenhair, grub and bird's nest ferns, and *Tillandsia usneoides* (old man's beard). Growing in pots are succulents, white cyclamen and agave. In the industrial timber crate is a variety of native grasses such as *Lomandra* and red fountain grass.

Decoration
We used an outdoor cement statue of a toadstool next to the basin, and the soap mimics a crystal and sits on a broken piece of granite used as a soap dish. The circular vanity mirror is edged in bamboo, which has been stained matte black. A lovely piece of old, recycled hardwood is used across the tub to hold candles that resemble timber logs and bath-time lotions and potions.

Transterior elements

1. Solid cedar wood bathtub
2. Sharkskin wallpaper
3. Maidenhair green matte acrylic paint
4. Vertical garden blanket
5. Ferns and other greenery
6. Vintage green metal potting bench
7. Cowhides and a reindeer pelt
8. Outdoor statue of a toadstool
9. Soap mimics a crystal
10. Granite used as a soapdish
11. Old, recycled hardwood
12. Candles!

DINING ROOM

We wanted to create a sense of occasion in this dining room – something dark and moody, with a sleek interior but a soft, warm edge and a kind of 'craftedness' about it. Being a room in which people gather and break bread together, it was vital to create a feeling of welcome, with an attention to materiality and tactility.

Floors and walls
The floors are black oak parquetry laid in a herringbone pattern. A Belgian black sisal rug adds another layer of natural texture to the floor. We had fun with the walls, painting them in a horizontal stripe in shades of muted greens, going from dark to light in an ombre effect. From bottom to top, Dark Gully Green, Gully Green, Timberline and Olive Grove.

Plants
Two black, glossy-leaved rubber plants in pots sit like a pair of sentinels on either side of the dining setting.

Furniture
The round, solid timber table has open, square legs giving it a refined, contemporary edge, and its translucent chalk finish lightens the look while showing off the timber's beautiful grain. The Kiki dining chairs with their ash-finish timber frame and black leather seats have a sophisticated, eye-catching shape. The black timber Vaughan console table provides another spot for drinks, plates and glasses.

Lighting
A black bamboo pendant shade in a retro style, with an industrial bulb, hangs low above the table.

Accents
Autumnal persimmons act as natural placeholders on the table, and the black-and-white theme is continued through from the napery to the dinner plates and coffee cups.

Soft furnishings
We chose smart cotton placemats and napkins in a bold black-and-white tie-dye pattern.

Decoration
Earthy, antique terracotta urns and two large bird prints in black frames add some interest.

Transterior elements

1 Black oak parquetry
2 Belgian black sisal rug
3 Paint in shades of muted greens
4 Rubber plants
5 Solid timber table
6 Kiki dining chairs in an ash finish
7 Earthy, antique terracotta urns
8 Two large bird prints
9 Black bamboo pendant shade

LIVING ROOM

This elegant living room displays some fine design elements without appearing flashy or unfriendly. It is a fresh take on the traditional formal living room – livable luxury at its best. The natural, organic components in this interior scheme keep it grounded and help to set the timeless tone with a soothing palette of neutrals accented by dusty blues, pinks and sage greens.

Soft furnishings
Curtains make perfect room dividers. They're a great solution in an open-plan warehouse space as they instantly add softness and an acoustic quality. They also create a wonderful sense of verticality, which we've made the most of in our set location. These curtains are made of an oatmeal-colour linen and have a broad panel of dusky taupe velvet on the inside of the living room and an ice blue on the opposite side. The sofa is scattered with cushions made from vintage Japanese fabrics.

Floors and walls
The colour of the matte acrylic paint used on the walls is Waterfall and the floors are covered in a subtle dusky blue/green alligator-skin print carpet.

Accents
A number of Asian accents, such as the Chinese blue-and-white porcelain planter, vintage Japanese cushions and contemporary Vietnamese watercolours, complete the look.

Lighting
The single Goccia decorative glass pendant hangs low in the centre of the room, ethereal, light and as magical as a floating soap bubble.

Plants
Clumps of *Tillandsia usneoides* (old man's beard), an air plant that grows virtually anywhere, trail from the windows. A huge dried-out gum tree branch, a bold alternative to cut flowers which works in any room, sits in a blue-and-white porcelain jar. I am a fan of cut foliage as it is always available and free if you have a garden. A planter in the centre of the room holds a lush *Cordyline fruticosa* (castor oil fern).

Decoration
All-natural *objets d'art* include quartz and amethyst crystals, pink paper daisies in a concrete pot and chrysanthemum blooms in a vase. I love Jacqui Fink's robust, tactile chunky macramé wall hanging, the main feature of the room. It is so organic it almost looks like giant hand-woven clumps of bleached seaweed. The basket is also by Jacqui, and holds soft woollen throw rugs for when the temperature drops.

Furniture

The Motti modular sofa is sleek and elegant, sitting on delicate polished brass feet and upholstered in an ecru-coloured fabric. The coffee table/zen garden is a fabulous piece as it brings nature inside and has a dual purpose as a table and great conversational piece. The main body of the miniaturised garden is a boxed-in gravel garden with clumps of moss and baby's tears growing in it. These plants are often used in bonsai as they bring a sense of age and establishment into the garden, mimicking full-size, open gardens. The black timber ledge table that sits over the zen garden is handy for drinks and nibbles, flowers – such as these two stunning chrysanthemums – and other treasured objects, such as books and ornaments. Black-and-white painted Tonk stools clustered together and used as side tables are a natural, creative way to use recycled, solid timber logs.

Transterior elements

1. Alligator-skin print carpet
2. Air plant
3. Dried-out gum tree branch
4. Large planter
5. The coffee table/zen garden
6. Clumps of moss and baby's tears
7. Black timber ledge table
8. Chrysanthemums
9. Recycled timber stools
10. Oatmeal-coloured linen
11. Quartz and amethyst crystals, pink paper daisies
12. Large, organic macramé artpiece
13. Soft woollen throw rugs
14. Bubble-look glass pendant

LOFT

We decided to do an industrial style warehouse conversion, similar to a Brooklyn loft with the flowing aesthetics of a modern home. Its main features include exposed brick walls, large windows, black steel beams and concrete floors covered in colourful rugs. We thought it would be an interesting use of space to create a home office integrated into the space. Modern furnishings and warm, natural colours help create a softer, more inviting space that is not too edgy.

Floors and walls

Bare concrete floors are covered with several colourful rugs – a round shape for the living room and two oblong green ombre shaded rugs for the office space. The offices ones are turned end to end for an interesting effect. The flat wall is painted in Watermelon Margherita colour.

Plants

Giant bromeliads (*Vriesea platynema* x fosteriana) in an unusual vintage fluted pot, cardboard plant (*Zamia furfuracea*) in a huge terracotta pot, a large magnolia tree (*Michelia alba*) in a wood-fired, bronze colour cauldron bowl and two potted bonsai.

Furniture

Furnishings are a mix of contemporary pieces from the mid-century inspired JD Float lounge and JD Brickwood marble-topped coffee table to Staccato bookshelves that, if you had two or three, could act as a room divider. The Hoodie office desk is perfect for a collaborative workplace; the 'hood', woven in Australian bush materials and natural dyes, supplies gentle isolation while allowing for contact with the rest of the space through subtle translucency.

Soft furnishings

Soft furnishings are minimal. Sofas and chairs are upholstered in simple neutrals, the only accent being a teal cushion with printed foliage design and artist Regina Wilson's *Syaw (Fish Net)* digital print design on a linen throw.

Decoration
Flowers and fruit are in the form of distinctive artworks. Over-sized ceramic cherry sculptures by Brazilian artist Selma Abdon Calheira and a selection of beautiful floral paintings by Ali Wood are dotted around the room.

Lighting
Apart from the desk lamp, there's a single pendant by Yolngu weavers from Elcho Island Arts in beautiful berry tones using natural materials from the Aussie bush and vegetable dyes.

Accents
The accents in this room are definitely the Australian indigenous hand-crafted pieces, which combine traditional art forms with contemporary design to bring a refreshing, soulful and grounded-in-the-earth effect to the modern space.

Transterior elements

1. Indoor plants – large scale to keshiki bonsai
2. Yuta Badayala natural woven hoodie on desk and pendant light
3. Botanical begonia motif printed cushion and textural throw
4. Earthy coloured woollen rugs
5. Ali Wood floral paintings
6. Cherry sculptures
7. Timber furniture
8. Driftwood log coat hook
9. Beeswax candles

SPACE

B

Space B is in an open section of the warehouse under a bank of skylights running the length of the space, with a flat plain, rendered wall sectioned off by black steel beams. This area allowed us enough space to create a couple of inside-out zones; those rooms that are literally on the threshold of an outdoor area.

BEDROOM

This bedroom is a sanctuary of relaxed romance. We wanted to create a soothing retreat with organic touches and some 'wow' factor, which is delivered by the amazing, oversized floral digital wallpaper by Ellie Cashman. The blooms add a lovely touch of quaintness, while promoting a sense of intimacy and softness. The room mixes the modern with the rustic in a contemporary way, allowing the seemingly opposite styles to co-exist.

Floors and walls

Floors are whitewashed oak and walls are painted in the colour Watermark. Ellie Cashman's Dark Floral wallpaper is used for the feature wall behind the bedhead; it's so rich and sensual, evoking nature within the space. Light-coloured floors seemed a more relaxed choice for this room.

Plants

We've used epiphytes, or air plants, hung from the string of lights and collected in a shallow bowl on the console table. They don't need soil, as they grow on other plants, or sometimes other objects such as a building or fence, and derive moisture and nutrients from the air, rain and sometimes from debris around them. They are native to humid climates.

Decoration

Extra decoration is minimal as it is already integrated into the functional elements, especially the birch logs of the four-poster bed, the texture of the hemp throw and, of course, the wallpaper. You can imagine how luxurious the reindeer pelt would feel underfoot as you step out of bed! In countries like Lapland, reindeer are hunted for food, so the hide is a by-product that completes the sustainable recycling process. Just in case you were wondering.

Furniture

The handmade, white birch four-poster bed gives this room a magical and modern yet rustic aura. This effect is reflected in the copper Bell side table with smoky glass pedestal and the crisp white leather settee.

Soft furnishings

Smooth, inviting sheets of pure linen in white and blue/grey contrast perfectly with the texture of the chunky hemp throw rug on the rustic four-poster bed. A knife-pleated grey woollen throw on the white leather daybed is a contemporary contrast to the cottage-style throw. A collection of rust-coloured throw cushions are piled on the daybed; one in plush elephant cord while others have digitally printed designs of a woven basket, woven leather and wood grain.

Lighting

A single pendant light of caged copper dangles from the ceiling and an LED string of the tiniest fairy lights hangs in a criss-cross over the bed. Dangling from the fairy lights are battery-operated LED Japanese-style paper lanterns. String lights and lanterns are a great way to introduce an alfresco outdoor feeling into your home interior.

Accents

The feature accents in this interior scheme are the clutch of interesting textures that weave through, creating a cohesive look, from the bark of the white birch to the digitally printed wood grain, basket weave and woven strips of leather on the cushions.

Transterior elements

1. Floral wallpaper
2. Limed floorboards
3. Birch log four-poster bed
4. Reindeer pelt on the floor
5. Leather and timber daybed
6. Linen bedlinen
7. Chunky knit hemp blanket
8. Basket-weave, wood-weave and leather-weave cushions
9. Airplants
10. Copper accent on bedside tables
11. LED party lights and Japanese lanterns

KIDS' BEDROOM

We knew we wanted to include a kids' room and thought it would be more fun if it was a shared room. I know that for many of you, room-sharing may not be your preference, but I honestly think it's a lovely, healthy thing for young kids to share a room. We've also given you a second option on how you could position the beds within the space; both ways work well.

Floors and walls
We left the concrete floors pretty bare, just adding a couple of round jute rugs in a mix of natural and bright colours. The walls are painted in Watermark, and the back wall has a zany zigzag border in Evergreen. The border could be a reference to the spikes along the spine and tail of a dinosaur or alligator, or it could be an ant's view of blades of grass . . . what you perceive is all up to the imagination!

Plants
The cactus is a playful, quirky shape that intrigues children and teaches them that not everything is to be touched – it's a lesson I never forgot!! And the philodendron is the perfect indoor plant, because it needs little light, takes a lot of neglect and is tough and long-lasting with basic care.

Soft furnishings
Brightly coloured cotton bedlinen in fun prints lightens up the grey flannel beds, as do the accent cushions, throw rugs and patchwork quilts.

Decoration
We've used a tree branch painted in random black-and-white stripes mounted on the wall to hang things. Treasured possessions and familiar pieces become the decorative elements in a child's room. Furniture arrangement, colour scheme and personal items on display act as decoration and give plenty of info about the little people who live there.

Accents
We've used a mixture of interesting framed, vintage and modern art prints around the room, as well as a Natalie Miller tapestry. Similar in concept (but not aesthetic!), to the ribbons kids win at sports carnivals, the oversized decorative rosettes dotted around the room are another lovely accent as rosettes suggest winning or achieving something significant.

Furniture
The vintage-inspired Charlie beds upholstered in grey flannel and perched on tapered timber feet are a smart and unexpected look for kids' beds. They don't look childish, they suit both girls and boys and they work extremely well paired with bedlinen in bright, clashing colours. The Archie table and chair set, colour box desk, clear acrylic Kartell stool and polka dot–upholstered stool are all functional pieces that look good and lack the cartoon-like quality of the awful brightly coloured plastic furniture usually used for kids' rooms. I much prefer proper furniture made from warm, nurturing natural materials for children.

Lighting
An Applicata ball pendant lamp hangs between the beds from the branch mounted on the wall.

Transterior elements

1. Concrete floors
2. Playful decorative spikes, depicting a dinosaur or alligator
3. Choice of paint colours
4. Cactus
5. Beds upholstered in grey flannel and perched on tapered timber feet
6. Fun animal, bird and fish prints
7. Branch painted in random black-and-white stripes
8. Tapestry by Natalie Miller

KITCHEN/ DINING

This is one of my favourite room sets as it shows a cross-section of different areas of the home – the kitchen/dining room and the flow through into an outdoor area. The interior flow of a home – in other words, the way rooms and spaces connect – is so important. This space has been planned to encourage an alfresco lifestyle. A deck, courtyard or patio connected to your kitchen and dining area is the most immediate way of bringing the outdoors in and a great feature when it comes to entertaining. We create many spaces that focus on the indoor/outdoor flow – it is a key feature of our design philosophy.

Floors and walls
Floorboards are Dusk Oak in the interior and there's a lovely textured large grey limestone paver, Gris San Vicente, flamed, in the courtyard. The walls are painted in Watermark, with a rusty, burnt orange chalkboard paint used as a message panel on the wall separating the kitchen from the dining area.

Plants
There is a large mop top *Acacia cognata* 'Waterfall' in the courtyard, a *Begonia rex* in the integrated planter bench and *Acacia cognata* 'Waterfall' and ZZ plant hanging in the kitchen.

Furniture
It's hard to beat wood as a material to work with. I can't get enough of it; it's my favourite medium when it comes to designing my own furniture collections. I love its warm tones and the beauty of the natural grain, and when used in designs that show off its natural texture, it's an irresistible recipe for success in interiors. There's a lot of timber in this living space, from vintage distressed pieces to modern designer pieces such as the Studioilse dining setting designed by Ilse Crawford. An innovative piece is the JD Avalon Integrated Planter Bench where plants merge with furniture.

Soft furnishings
An A&Co. Sandrift hall runner tracks along the border between inside and outside, and connects the kitchen area. Painterly cushions cosy up the dining bench and integrated planter bench.

Lighting
A casual cluster of Yuta Badayala hand-woven pendant light fittings are bunched together over the dining setting, creating a beguiling scene. The earthy colours and textures of the pendants come from the natural dyes mixed with dried grasses and feathers. They look like a bunch of upside-down baskets.

Decoration

Copper ceramic fruit sculptures by Brazilian artist Selma Abdon Calheira are mixed in with various pieces of crockery, glassware, cooking moulds, colourful, jugs, platters and Dinosaur Designs resin bowls and platters.
The mix of crockery on display in the pigeonhole-style timber shelves is kept to a simple colour palette of white, cream and a bright pop of yellow. This helps make the space feel cohesive and not too cluttered, even though you've got quite a bit happening on those shelves.

Accents

The accent in this area is on mixing the old with the new. I find spaces that stick rigidly to a single style or period really boring, to be honest. We've mixed new, designer pieces with vintage, second-hand and antique pieces, in everything from the furniture to the collection of art, crockery and glassware. This immediately creates an inviting, lived-in, eclectic look. In real life you are always blending inherited pieces with sentimental importance with newer items – that's what makes your home uniquely your own! You have to work on getting the balance right though, so the room looks elegant and not just a haphazard mix of junk.

Transterior elements

1. Alfresco lifestyle deck, courtyard or patio connected to your kitchen and dining area
2. Floorboards of a natural colour
3. Grey limestone pavers
4. Plants both inside and out
5. Avalon Integrated Planter Bench
6. Copper ceramic fruit sculptures
7. Hand-woven pendant light fittings

SUNROOM

If you grew up in Australia, you probably have memories of sleepovers in your nana's sunroom. It was that room tacked onto the back of homes to create a bit of extra space, often used as an extra bedroom for visitors. Sunrooms are either attached to, or integrated into, the architecture of the home. They don't have to be at the back of the property – they should be wherever there is the greatest exposure to sunshine and the natural landscape. They usually have a lot of glazing while still being undercover and sheltered from the elements. These days a sunroom is more commonly referred to as a patio or porch. I have always loved the idea of sunrooms and conservatories and think it's high time they had a renaissance! This is our take on the modern sunroom.

Floors and walls
We cut a narrow, horizontal opening into one of the walls to allow plant foliage to creep in. We also painted that wall in Porter's Rock Salt, and the adjacent wall in Watermark. The floor of the sunroom is made from Lavagrigia sawn (ignimbrite) tiles, and the grey continues outside with the outdoor pavers in Gris San Vicente, flamed limestone. A Belgian grey sisal rug with a bound edge softens the sitting area in the sunroom and also helps to define the undercover area from the open area.

Plants
Many plants are used, including agave, black mondo grass, Boston fern, philodendron, black rubber plant, agave, fishbone ferns and rhapis palms.

Furniture
We used a combination of materials in the furniture, mixing metal with wood, so there were different visual weights. The metal furniture like the Seb chair and Jil table are light and airy, yet have a bold geometry to them. The timber furniture is weighty, and the large Nomah armchairs with upholstered cushions in a slub linen create a comfy lounge room outside. At the threshold between the undercover and open areas, we suspended a 'thinking' swing to add an element of fun.

Soft furnishings
The upholstered cushion on the Seb chairs is stitched to mimic the geometric design of the chair frame. Cushions screen-printed with natural motifs in black and white, such as Garden Rose and Wattle, add another layer of comfort and botanical beauty. A canvas ottoman digitally printed with a mountain scene is a great occasional seat for a casual setting like this.

Decoration
We've used a combination of pots made of rough textured pottery and smooth, modern metal troughs. Stephen Ormandy's *Primary* oil painting relates beautifully to the bold geometry of the furniture, acting as a focal point that adds some unexpected pops of colour to make you pay attention!

Accents

We created a magical, floating flower decoration from an old zinc washtub. In Asian countries, many people use water and flower bowls like this to introduce beauty and a feeling of peace and happiness into their homes. You can use flowers, petals, leaves and floating candles in this way to great effect.

Transterior elements

1. Sunrooms are either attached to or integrated into the architecture of the home
2. Horizontal opening into one of the walls to allow plant foliage to creep in
3. Lavagrigia sawn (ignimbrite) stone tiles
4. Gris San Vicente, flamed limestone pavers
5. Belgian grey sisal rug
6. A variety of plants
7. Timber furniture
8. Combination of materials in the furniture, mixing metal with wood
9. Cushions screen-printed with flowers
10. Canvas ottoman printed with a mountain scene
11. Pots made of rough textured pottery
12. Metal troughs
13. Oil painting on linen
14. Floating flowers in an old zinc washtub

WORKROOM

We wanted to include a creative workroom that you might have at home. It should be inspiring and positive – your dream workspace. Again, we've set up this room to flow through to the outside, whether that be a garden, deck or courtyard. What could be more inspiring than to have nature close by?! The position of your work table is important, and we've given it top priority by placing it right in the middle of the room, as this is where you would spend most of your time. We imagine the creative person working here would need plenty of room to move around, so we tried to create a great flow.

ERMES
VIE

Floors and walls

We used Dusk Oak floorboards inside the workroom and Gris San Vicente, flamed limestone pavers for the outdoor area. To rev up the colour in this room we chose Porter's Panorama; it's the most beautiful cerulean shade. Certain colours stimulate the emotions; blue is meant to be soothing when used as the main colour in a room, and is also meant to be a productive colour for an office or workspace.

Accents

The distressed, white-painted, timber shutters make a lovely accent simply leaning against the walls. These timeless objects conjure up an alfresco atmosphere inside, and we've extended them from the interior to the outdoor area to create a sense of seamlessness. We've created an inspiration board of magazine tear sheets on the blue wall. Whenever I see other people's collections of what inspires them, I'm immediately inspired too. Mood or vision boards, and in this room's case, the inspiration tear sheets that have been stuck directly onto the blue wall, add so much spontaneity to this space. It's these touches that really express a person's warmth and personality in a home.

Furniture

An oversized trestle makes an ideal counter-height table. We took the stylised poppy design of the fabric on the outdoor cushions and digitally printed that onto the trestle worktop for a bit of fun and to carry the orange into the interior. Blue and orange is one of my favourite colour combinations. Although blue on its own is a calming, peaceful colour, when you combine it with orange, it's great for getting the creative juices flowing. As well as the white storage cabinets, there's a funky industrial stool and a slick black-and-white Audrey chair by Piero Lissoni for Kartell, which looks like a contemporary version of a timber chair with woven cane seat and back. There is a Scandi-style timber Nelson setting in the outside area, and the outdoor coffee table is made from squared-off hardwood logs.

Soft furnishings
Cushions on the Nelson setting are upholstered in a bright orange and white Poppy Major outdoor fabric from the Blume Collection by Signature Prints. A blue garden rose screen-printed cushion continues our blue-and-orange colour combination. There is a white cowhide on the floor of the workroom, dyed using the ancient Japanese shibori technique, a type of tie-dye using indigo dye.

Plants
A large bonsai *Adenanthos sericeus* (woolly bush) planted with *Viola hederacea* (native violet), begonia, yucca, hanging pots of *Solanum jasminoides* (potato vine).

Lighting
A vintage bulb is suspended with a vintage, rusted metal, pendant shade, adding an industrial and textural element to the room.

Decoration
There are two lithographs by Kozyndan on the walls. The one on the left, *Vegans*, depicts manatees with rabbits riding on them with blue hydrangeas in the background. The one on the right, *Hunters*, has great white sharks with cats riding on them against a background of pink chrysanthemums. I love the inherent sense of fun in these artworks and the way the artist expresses a unique view of nature.

On another wall is a collection of mid-century modern framed prints by Chris Turnham, *Eames House* and *Palm Print 1* and *2*. All things mid-century modern inspire me, and these prints really remind me of the architecture and vibrant nature of LA. The begonia plant on the table is in a handmade Lazy Season pot, which is a limited edition design object. The begonia is self-watering and has a cute bronze prop to enable it to be placed at any angle. Dotted around the room are many decorative objects and art pieces, such as the pair of porcelain roses in terracotta pots.

Transterior elements

1. Room to flow through to the outside
2. Oak floorboards
3. Blue walls
4. Plenty of plants
5. An oversized trestle
6. Poppy design of the fabric
7. Industrial stool
8. Chair with woven cane seat and back
9. Scandinavian-style timber setting
10. Coffee table from squared-off hardwood logs
11. White cowhide on the floor of the workroom
12. Artworks with animals and palms
13. Decorative porcelain roses in terracotta pots

TRANSTERIOR LIVING

TRANSTERIOR IN ACTION

In this final chapter of our book I've brought together a few examples of quintessential transterior homes. Each one is an ode to nature in its own individual way, and tries to keep nature as close as possible in a number of ways. That could be through the materials used, or by the design that allows direct access to the elements of nature. It could also be through the use of interior gardens, or motifs and other representations of nature in day-to-day living spaces.

I really believe that it's architecture and interior design that hold the vision and philosophy of transterior. The eternal values and a sense of soulfulness that come from transterior will ultimately endure well and be truly significant. When you purposely set out to create transteriors – to connect and integrate nature into a house – there is a special quality to that work, and it imparts a certain grace, style and life force. The desire to create beauty and commune with nature through transterior design feels almost like a spiritual experience for me. Nature is my greatest inspiration, so I guess that makes sense. As you look through each of these homes, I think you will get an appreciation of what I'm trying to say. In living close to nature we hopefully intuit something of the ancient wisdom of the earth and are better for it.

This impressive, living, breathing, vertical garden is a sculptural work of art. It is a breath of fresh air – literally – in the Paris apartment, as the wall of green works to generate oxygen, cleaning the air around it. How could you *not* feel delighted living with this inside your living room every day?!

MOSS RESIDENCE

Sydney, Australia

Dear friends of ours, Lata and Bill Moss, recently moved into their new apartment in a distinguished building on Sydney Harbour. The apartment is situated with spectacular, panoramic harbor views, incorporating the Sydney Opera House and Royal Botanic Gardens, which make for the most incredible, jaw-dropping vista to live with.

MOSS RESIDENCE

The Mosses commissioned Lisa Saville and Steven Isaacs of Saville Architects to renovate the apartment interior with a general and open brief giving minimal, specific requests.

The existing apartment had nothing transterior about it. It felt claustrophobic, with pokey rooms and walls at odd angles. It really had very little relationship with the sweeping curved external glass façade or the extraordinary view beyond. They've transformed the home entirely, creating one large, open, light and bright space with a strong connection to the outside with its iconic view. I've rarely stood in a space that made me feel so connected to its surroundings.

After the existing apartment was gutted, the concept for the interior design was to insert some fluidly curved joinery pods to house the bathrooms, laundry and services as well as giving the actual space a sculpted, arty effect. The soft curve of this joinery mimics the curve of the exterior of the building, as well as enabling the family perfectly seamless access throughout the home. The interior curves also help to create a wonderful sense of arrival as you journey from the front door into a larger space; you get the feeling you are being drawn out from the small entry foyer, towards the light and the view in the main living space. It's a great example of Frank Lloyd Wright's 'compress and release' theory. The entry way feels compressed and then as you move towards the living area, there is a wonderful feeling of release.

One of my favourite aspects of the design is the colour palette. Creamy white was chosen to further enhance the feeling of airy openness and act as a conduit to the Opera House with a strong nod to its milky sails. The copper accents are a lovely, earthy touch and were chosen to bring a bit of life and contrast to the all-white space. I love copper –

it's one of my favourite transterior materials. It has great richness and depth, and I can imagine how beautifully it will evolve and change over time, adding its warm patina to enrich the space as it distresses.

Most of the timber you see in the apartment was sourced from trees that fell down during violent storms on Bill and Lata's country property. I thought it was a wonderful personal touch to recycle their beloved trees and bring them inside their city dwelling. The timber is a great contrast to the other elements and provides a warm and natural touch, especially with its added emotional value.

This apartment is such a wonderful example of a transterior home because the space is all about an abundance of natural light, the connection to water, the Opera House, Botanic Gardens and, of course, the Harbour Bridge and views of harbour life. When you're in this space you don't feel like you're in a man-made structure at all. With its organic, sinuous spaces, it feels as if you are living inside an enormous, pearly sea shell.

This type of interior represents a fresh, modern take on contemporary housing. The style is open, approachable, and unassuming, yet with a distinctly natural and unique, earth-house vocabulary.

HOUSE ON A DUNE

Harbour Island, The Bahamas

I'm sure I'm not alone when I say I would love to live in a house like this. In a time where architecture can sometimes be over complicated, House on a Dune is elegant in its simplicity, and is designed to enhance one's experience of the beautiful island nature that envelops the site. It has been built to inspire and make the most of pleasurable moments of living within the space.

HOUSE ON A DUNE

It embodies a refreshing, less invasive, primitive architecture of simplistic form utilising ecologically sensitive materials within the overall design. The interiors are elemental and liveable, free of clutter and unnecessary detail, which allows for a more powerful and dramatic connection to place and time and, most importantly, to nature. All mod cons of high-tech living are hidden away, adding even more to the sense of connection with place.

Visionary architect Chad Oppenheim's incredible waterfront dwelling is a true manifestation of a transterior. Inspired by the work of conceptual artist James Turrell, retractable glass walls on the east and west sides of the living area frame views of ocean, jungle and sky, while allowing for light and air to flow through the home to create a comfortable, well-ventilated dwelling. The central space of the house is basically an open breezeway that provides access across various zones. Contained within this pavilion space are the living and dining areas that sweep onto sizeable terraces well sheltered from the elements by generous extensions of the gabled roof. The kitchen and four bedrooms are plainly set around the main pavilion.

Timber is the primary natural material and its inherent sincerity and environmental sensitivity is at the core of the design's vernacular. Other materials used include concrete blocks, recycled cedar, recycled ipe timber and milk paint. The roof made of cedar shakes is traditional to the area, similar to those found on centuries-old island houses.

House on a Dune represents the architect's signature style, which is to create socially and environmentally conscious architecture. Here, Oppenheim has transformed the prosaic into the poetic, drawing on the site's inherent power through passion and sensitivity towards both man and nature. Through this alchemy, transterior spaces are created.

ISHIBE HOUSE

Konan, Shiga, Japan

Here's a wonderful example of transterior design from Japan. It's a seemingly humble abode, yet deeply rich in its connection to nature. ALTS Design's clients, a married couple in their twenties with one child, wanted to live in a renovated warehouse.

ISHIBE HOUSE

They loved the contemporary style of living space a warehouse has to offer, with its industrial character, textured, distressed walls, high ceilings and skylights. However, it can be expensive and difficult to convert an open warehouse into a warm and comfortable home, often costing as much as a new building. The couple decided to build a brand new house, which feels like a renovated warehouse, working in all the different productive open areas you might find in an industrial space. The main difference to your average warehouse, though, is that it feels a lot more cosy and warm. This is partly due to the use of natural timber throughout.

In the middle of the building, the architects constructed a white cube and put rooms that needed privacy inside that. The rest of the house is split-level, with open spaces that the family can arrange as they wish to suit their lifestyle. Exposed oak beams give a tree house feel to this industrial home and also add a warm, rustic element. Clever use of lauan plywood off-cuts are used for flooring and to clad walls.

The architects' central philosophy is connection to nature through their designs, and their approach to each project stems from this. Of course, each and every project is a unique result with richness and diversity of its own. Yes, this is a newly constructed durable, industrial type of building from the exterior. But, in addition, the architects have gone to great lengths to make it feel as if it has been there for decades, incorporating all the imperfections that go along with that. And, as the family lives there, adding even more depth to it over the years to come, it will only improve steadily with age.

TRUCK WORKS

The interior of this serene dwelling displays so much balance and harmony in its design that, to me, it's almost like a meditation in and of itself. It's a humble and natural home that seems to have a firm foothold in its own cosy corner of the world.

TRUCK WORKS

KOFUNAKI HOUSE

Omihachiman, Shiga, Japan

This charming Japanese house is an exquisite example of bringing the outside in. Even though it's quite a simple urban home, it's so inspiring to me that they've integrated nature right through the very heart of the architecture.

KOFUNAKI HOUSE

The placement of the whimsical interior gardens is so reverent and meaningful; the living plants are dotted around the house like precious totems. Japan is one of my favourite countries to visit for inspiration; nature and the change of seasons is so integral to the Japanese aesthetic, and is very much an influential part of their life. It's obvious that nature is held in the highest regard – it can be seen, for instance, in the way they landscape their gardens or express themselves through the art of bonsai. Perhaps that may stem from the fact that many of them live in small places well away from wilderness areas.

The house that Sumiou Mizumoto and Yoshitaka Kuga from ALTS Design Office have designed is a celebration of the natural landscape. By creating a building with plenty of natural light, in which plants are able to thrive, there is an immediate connection between inside and outside. On top of that, the spaces seem to contain a tangible life force.

The architects explain the concept for this design. 'We decided that this theme of ours, living in woods in woods in a home.' In other words, we all live in nature in the greater world, but the inhabitants of this home live with nature inside their own home. Nature, within and without.

This is a home that has been created to enable the inhabitants to experience nature and the changing seasons at close quarters. It's a habitat that has, according to the architects, 'the ability to soften a family's heart, and could grow up a family with woods. It is the proposal of a rich new life where people enjoy space and enjoy a life, it is a place in woods.'

Need we say more ...

What is the secret to a beautiful, homey home? Comfort needs to be subtly woven into the aesthetic design, and the qualities of luxury should be disguised as simplicity and a sense of being uncomplicated. At the end of the day it's not really what's in a room and how it's furnished that makes it attractive, it is a spirit that infuses the space. This home has that spirit in spades!

LA MUNA

Aspen, Colorado, USA

This wonderful house is not only an exemplary illustration of a transterior home, but also a lovely example of how humble architecture, when at its most uncontrived, feels like it's suspended in time between the past and present.

LA MUNA

Over the years, the house had undergone a number of changes that had hidden much of its beauty. Oppenheim Architecture carried out a complete renovation, including a minor addition, and in doing so, restored this rustic ski chalet with all its charming imperfections as a homage to the Japanese sensibility of *wabi sabi*.

Now clad in reclaimed local timber, stone, weathered steel and copper, this house makes minimal impact on natural resources and merges effortlessly with the forest, stream and mountains around it. Solar collectors provide energy needed for power and hot water, while extremely large operable panels of insulated glass open the house up to the amazing vista beyond, blurring the boundaries between inside and out – further enhancing the strong connection to nature and deep respect for a sense of place.

The interior palette of eggshell plaster walls, raw, silvery timbers, charcoal stained floors and crushed linen and leather-covered furnishings all underwrite and supply a feeling of comfort, a pure, unprocessed sense of monastic luxury. There is a stillness to *wabi sabi* and there's a tangible stillness with this interior. Even the sizeable artwork over the dining setting, made up of clumps of dried moss, pays tribute to the deep feeling that *wabi sabi* invokes.

The powerful transformation of this house expresses the majesty of the beautiful forest and mountain landscape surrounding it. The natural materials used in the architecture and the interior design exemplify a rustic charm of simplicity, purity and intimacy. It's a wonderful space to be in where you feel so in touch with the outer world and the changing seasons.

MAISON JMD

Paris, France

Thank goodness for the revolutionary, evolutionary work of the genius French landscape designer and botanist Patrick Blanc. He is the pioneer of the whole vertical garden movement sweeping through urban areas around the globe, greening the cities of the world, one building at a time.

MAISON JMD

I talk and write about Patrick's work on vertical gardens all the time because I am so inspired by his championing of this innovative game changer in the landscape industry. Inspired enough to become an advocate, I have now designed my own system for growing gardens vertically, the Vertical Greenwall Blanket (see page 36–37).

As long as you provide enough natural light, you can bring nature inside in abundance; the sheer magnificence of having a whole wall of garden is hard to beat. It is beautiful to live with, and will inspire you every day. You can see the power behind it when looking at this example. Try to imagine the space without the vertical garden – it just wouldn't be the same. The magic transterior quality would be negligible.

The apartment's owner, Jean-Marc Dimanche, and XY Architecture designed the building, which is on a narrow, six-metre-wide block in the heart of Paris. Its glass façade rises seventeen metres, and thank goodness for that, because this is the vital access to natural light plants need. To correct the absence of real nature on this site, Jean-Marc installed many small outdoor spaces, but it was only when he met Patrick Blanc that the idea of installing an entire garden wall in the generously proportioned, double-height living room was born. This is a stunning example of a living, growing, tactile garden wall. I love the plant palette used as the foliage is varied, textural and offers many shades of green to please the eye.

The interiors are a mix of dark and cosy, almost cave-like rooms and lovely open areas full of natural light from the glass façade. When the owner bought the land, he found three amazing tree trunks on site, too beautiful to waste. These have been incorporated into the living room, where the three silent sentinels are positioned in one corner of the sitting room. A perfect transterior touch.

RIDGE ROAD RESIDENCE

Melbourne, Australia

A dramatic site characterised by a steep slope and a single windswept tea tree strongly informed Studiofour's design vision for this project. The designers have created a transterior form that not only respects its natural surroundings and draws it inside at every opportunity, but also allows their clients to interact closely with it on many levels.

RIDGE ROAD RESIDENCE

The home owners wanted to move to the coast to enjoy a change in pace and lifestyle, as well as be able to have a greater connection with the landscape in ways that were not possible, or even contemplated, in their former house in the suburbs.

Outstanding features of this house are the varying levels of interaction and connection with the landscape, both real and perceived, that drive all aspects of the transterior design. That includes the channelled views of the horizon upon entry, the double-height picture window that captures the full proportion of the tea tree, and the direct and intimate connection with nature provided by the low-level decks.

The camouflaged dwelling is hard to get a glimpse of through the surrounding vegetation, and where it can be seen, it blends into the landscape. The black timber cladding and dark reflective glass certainly help in this regard. In fact, the house is so perfect for its surrounds that it dematerialises, as the landscape overpowers the interior in the nicest possible way.

The interiors have the most exquisite lightness of being, so simple and restrained that the shelter provided indoors feels comparable to a light, transparent veil between the inside and out. It's a perfect example of the magical alchemy of transterior.

The designers explain that, as with all their projects, it was important to 'capture the genius loci ... and to make the most of any site's weakness'. By genius loci, they mean the atmosphere of a specific place.

I think this is a wonderful way to architecturally exhibit a transterior space, as with every aspect of the design process they have endeavoured to connect with the prevailing natural character and atmosphere of the special piece of nature on which it is perched.

I believe that always providing
a connection to nature is the key
to acquiring that special energy.

SPRING RESTAURANT

London, England

Spring is a serene restaurant space set in iconic Somerset House, in the heart of London. Somerset House is a large, serious, neo-classical building situated on the south side of the Strand in central London, overlooking the River Thames, just east of Waterloo Bridge. The Spring dining space is a breath of fresh air.

SPRING RESTAURANT

Originally from Australia, Skye Gyngell is now one of Britain's most respected chefs. Her sister, Briony Fitzgerald, designed the interior of her new restaurant. Skye wanted something quite different from the masculine restaurants in the West End. 'Although they look wonderful and I could see the temptation to take the space in that direction, it wouldn't have felt right,' she says. 'Women largely ran the project and Spring itself and I really wanted to celebrate that. I wanted a strong yet very feminine space.'

Australian interior designer Briony Fitzgerald is renowned for her clever use of colour. She has an incredible sensibility for combining not only colour but also a carefully curated palette of materials to create genuinely happy spaces. In putting together the concept for Spring, she kept in mind Skye's vision, which was for a convivial space. 'A space that felt warm and inviting, a more feminine experience that would engage the guest within – a welcome contrast to traditional English restaurants of days gone by,' says Briony.

She also explains the relationship between the food and materials. 'Skye's food has a natural simplicity, it is honest food, and she only uses the best seasonal produce. This ethos is echoed in the natural materials used throughout the restaurant: leather, marble, timber, paper, stone, waxed plaster, brass. We wanted to source bespoke pieces made with integrity, which utliised traditional materials and showcased the exquisite craftsmanship worthy of the building.'

The design has a strong connection to nature and I especially love the atrium, which gives Spring an airy feeling. Originally an open courtyard, collaborator Stuart Forbes designed a metal and glass roof that allows light to pour in. Along with its waxed gunnera leaf plaster walls and some olive trees, it helps create the impression of a conservatory.

CHERRYFIELDS

Somerset County, New Jersey, USA

My dear friends Geoffrey Ross and John Dransfield are the amazing designers behind well-known US home furnishings brand Dransfield & Ross. I have had the pleasure of visiting their unique and exquisite home in New Jersey and knew straight away that we had to shoot it for this book.

CHERRYFIELDS

I really love this old house because it's evolved over a long period and there's a story behind it. It was originally comprised of two simple farmhouses built around 1804. The property was eventually sold to two sisters, who, in about 1929, commissioned architect A. Musgrave Hyde to connect the two existing cottages and create the sprawling neo-Georgian home that is Cherryfields today.

Geoffrey and John moved into the house in 2006 with their beloved Great Dane, India. Although they were slightly intimidated about making any sweeping changes because of its 'storied design legacy', they quickly came to realise they needed a design that would suit today's lifestyle.

The couple describe their style as idiosyncratic and I would agree. To me there is a strong connection to nature in many ways, from the framed geographical maps on the walls and motifs of flora and fauna used everywhere to the over-abundance of natural materials and artefacts as well as the man-made articles resembling natural objects.

'We rarely buy flowers and, even though we have flowers in the garden, we most often use culled weeds or out-of-place saplings for arrangements,' says Geoffrey. 'I love the opportunity to look at invasive weeds from our garden in a new context. You would be surprised how striking many can be.' I couldn't agree more!

Geoffrey and John are both fond of inviting the outdoors inside and value their connection to the natural world. 'For a fall party once, we covered the living room floor with leaves raked up from the lawn,' says Geoffrey. 'It was striking, economical and memorably beautiful.' I'm smiling to myself as I write, because we did the same thing for a media launch party a few years ago. Great minds and all that.

Geoffrey and John are masters of the mix. The interior is a refreshing combination of seemingly disparate furnishings and decoration, yet somehow it all works. Some rooms are cottagey, while others feel stately, and there are lots of earthy touches everywhere. A house of many moods, there is always ebb and flow as it is constantly evolving.

JASPER CONRAN COUNTRY
THE COMPLETE COLLECTION OF
ANTIQUITIES
TASCHEN
RICHARD NEUTRA

POM
PEI
BOSSERT · FOLK ART OF EUROPE
PAISLEY PATTERNS VALERIE REILLY

The bones of this charming house lends itself well to the art of furnishing. Rich and elaborate textiles are used extravagantly; tables are full of ornaments and decoration in high-ceilinged rooms. Overall there is an atmosphere of restfulness and refinement.

Nadine

Jamie's muse and fearless creative director, Nadine Bush, came from a very different design background. She started working on the editorial side of fashion at *Sheila* magazine. Her career in design began when she and her family bought a fashion boutique, Chameleon, in Sydney's Double Bay. She supplied fashionistas with all the right apparel and accoutrements and soon became known for her courageous style and pioneering design sensibility.

Jamie first met Nadine on 11 February, 1998, when she was decorating editor at *Belle* magazine, one of Australia's premier design publications. She had been in that role for eight years, and he had noted that her contributions were distinctive and always original. Jamie says 'After years of me begging her to come and work with me she finally agreed, and started in 2003. Nadine has been one of the driving forces and key influences behind our "design DNA", pouring her creative energy into each and every one of our design projects. She has an impeccable sense of style and the unique ability to sift through the mundane, unearthing the unusual, the raw luxury that might go unnoticed by other eyes.'

Jamie

International award-winning designer and author Jamie Durie started his design practice in 1998. Since then, he and his team at Durie Design have received more than 33 international design awards, including in 2014, a gold award for his Elle Ecrite Desk and silver award for the Rainbow Modulare at the London Design Awards and, in the same year, the New York Design Award for the Tubular Chair, a dining chair.

Jamie's latest collection for renowned Milan-based Italian furniture manufacturer RIVA1920 launched at Salone del Mobile, Milan, in 2013. Since then, the collection has doubled with the Elle Ecrite Desk being commissioned by all RIVA1920 USA retail outlets with an outdoor range due to be released soon.

Jamie splits his time between design studios in Sydney and Los Angeles, and has worked on many hotels, resorts and commercial projects in seventeen countries around the world.

This book is dedicated to
Noelene Ratnayake and Natalie McCurry.
Forever in our hearts.

Acknowledgements

Julie Gibbs for your discerning guidance and support, but also for your impeccable taste. Oh yes, and those fabulous pots of tea!

Nick Bowers for your beautiful photography – it's always a pleasure working with you.

Tonya McCahon, thanks for all your lovely photography and your patience.

Evi O. for being so much fun to work with and making the pages look so darn good.

Nicole Abadee for helping us get organised and all the valuable advice – really . . . thank you!

Katrina O'Brien, you kept us to our course in your lovely calm way, 'Zen Goddess', and Leta Keens for your incredible attention to detail.

All our wonderful contributing photographers from around the globe – the inimitable Richard Powers, Jennifer Soo, Armelle Habib, Daniel Shipp, Edward Addeo, Brent Darby, Brett Boardman and Simon Kenny, to name a few.

Thanks to all the incredible architects and designers who allowed their work to be showcased here.

To Briony Fitzgerald and Skye Gyngell, Bill and Lata Moss, John Dransfield and Geoffrey Ross for allowing us into your incredible places.

A special, special thank you to Justin Weiley from The Furniture Courier Specialist and Phil Bennet and his team for all your careful, hard work.

We'd like to thank our amazing A-team at Durie Design – David Knott, Desmond Stock, Alinta Lim, Ben Ashton, Deanne Curry and Paulina Frankowski. You guys completely rock and we would be lost without you, especially for all your support during our shoot days for Chapter Five!

Love Nadz and Jamie x

Ohh, and PS, Nads, thank you for being my muse for more than 18 years now. Apart from the incredible human being that we all know you are, you are also blessed with stunning taste and sensibility.
J x

Stockist list

P i – Rug
Armadillo, **armadillo-co.com**

P 3 – Brickwood coffee table and Bolo lamp – Jamie Durie, **jamiedurie.com**

Artworks
Jamie Durie/The Canvas Workshop
jamiedurie.com

Sheepskin – Hides Of Excellence
hidesofexcellence.com.au

Planters – Evie Group, **eviegroup.com**

Cowhide rug – NSW Leather Co, **leatherco.com.au**

Sofa – Life Interiors, **lifeinteriors.com.au**

P 4 – Dining Setting
Cosh Living, **coshliving.com.au**

Teal planter – Bo Concept, **boconcept.com**

Tumbler – Top 3 By Design, **top3.com.au**

P 5 – Ethnicraft oak shelving
Click On Furniture, **clickonfurniture.com.au**

Bolo lamp – Jamie Durie, **jamiedurie.com**

P 45 – Cushion
Bonnie & Neil, **bonnieandneil.com.au**

Bedspread
Pony Rider, **ponyrider.com.au**

P 49 – Rug
Armadillo, **armadillo-co.com**

P 53 – Rose painting – Marcella Kaspar, **marcellakasparart.com**

P 58 – Rug
Armadillo, **armadillo-co.com**

P 90 – Indigenous artwork
The Artery, **artery.com.au**

P 95 – Painted ceramic plates
Susan Hipgrave, **susanhipgrave.com**

P 101 – Floral headdress
Sami Sweeting, **sami-sweeting.com**

P 104 – artwork, cushions, and sofa
Jamie Durie/The Canvas Workshop
jamiedurie.com

Wallpaper – Louise Jones 'Tropical' printed by Rebel Walls/Scandinavian wallpaper, **rebelwalls.com.au**

Side table – Evie Group, **eviegroup.com**

Candle – Top 3 By Design, **top3.com.au**

Sheepskin throw – Hides Of Excellence
hidesofexcellence.com.au

Pendant light
Domayne, **domayneonline.com.au**

Green vase
Bo Concept, **boconcept.com**

Rug – Eden Gardens, **edengardens.com.au**

P 109, 119, 125, 131, 137, 143 – Fabric samples – South Pacific Fabrics, **southpacificfabrics.com**

Paint and timber flooring samples
Porter's Paints, **porterspaints.com**

Tiles – Bisanna Tiles, **bisanna.com.au**

Rugs – The Rug Collection, **therugcollection.com.au;**
Tibet, **tibetsydney.com**

P 109 – Small mother of pearl spoon
The Bay Tree, **thebaytree.com.au**

White ceramic bowl
Planet, **planetfurniture.com.au**

P 110–112 – 'MamaPapa House', **mamapapa.com.au**

P 116 – Small glass containers
The Bay Tree, **thebaytree.com.au**

P 119 – Rug sample
Tibet, **tibetsydney.com**

Vinyl linoleum flooring samples
Tarkett, **tarkett.com.au**

P 125 –
Nush 2015; *Night's Tale* 2012 floral paintings – Marcella Kaspar, **marcellakasparart.com**

Rug samples – The Rug Collection, **therugcollection.com.au**
Tibet, **tibetsydney.com**

P 131 –
Rug samples – The Rug Collection, **therugcollection.com.au**
Tibet, **tibetsydney.com**

Ping Pong Bat landscape 5 –
Paul Ryan –
Olsen Irwin, **olsenirwin.com**

P 137 –
Inferno's Ghost 2015 – Sophie Cape
Olsen Irwin, **olsenirwin.com**

Brass dishes
Planet, **planetfurniture.com.au**

Plaster moulding
Bailey Interiors, **baileyinteriors.com.au**

Chandelier crystal drop sample
Chandeliers To Die For, **chandeliers.net.au**

P 143 – Background rug
Cadry's, **cadrys.com.au**

Floral rug – Tibet, **tibetsydney.com**
Hydrangeas in a Vase artwork
Ali Wood, **aliwoodart.com**

P 146
Jamie Durie for Riva 1920 Rope Stool
Jamie Durie, **jamiedurie.com**

Sheepskin – Hides Of Excellence, **hidesofexcellence.com.au**

Cushions – Jamie Durie/The Canvas Workshop, **jamiedurie.com**

P 148 – *Two Tanks* artwork
Becky Gibson, **beckygibson.net**

P 150–151 – Pale green bedlinen
Koskela, **koskela.com.au**

Cushion and embroidered bed cover
Planet, **planetfurniture.com.au**

Painting – Marcella Kaspar, **marcellakasparart.com**

Reindeer pelt
Shades Of Pale, Hunters Hill NSW
02 9817 4310

P 152–153

Butterfly resin pendants and resin plates
Dinosaur Designs, **dinosaurdesigns.com.au**

Printed underplates – Bonnie and Neil, **bonnieandneil.com.au**

Placemats – Armadillo, **armadillo-co.com**

Banksia aromatherapy pod
Planet, **planetfurniture.com.au**

P 154 –155 – Artwork
Azuma Makoto, **azumamakoto.com**

P 157 – Rug
Armadillo, **armadillo-co.com**

P 168 – Hanging jelly planters
Angus & Celeste, **angusandceleste.com**

P 170–171 – Staghorns
staghorn.net.au

P 176–177 – Terrariums
Justine Rose, **justinerose.com.au**

P 178–179 – Interior by Hecker Guthrie
Pale green bedlinen
Koskela, **koskela.com.au**

Cushion and embroidered bed cover
Planet, **planetfurniture.com.au**

Painting – Marcella Kaspar, **marcellakasparart.com**

Reindeer pelt
Shades Of Pale, Hunters Hill NSW
02 9817 4310

P 180 – Flower stand
Parterre Garden, **parterre.com.au**

P 181 – Flower arrangement
Jardine Botanic, **jardinebotanic.com.au**

P 183 – Artworks Tracey Deep

P 184–185 – All furniture and lighting
Jamie Durie, **jamiedurie.com**

P 186–187
Jil coffee table and Mini Softline planter – Tait, **madebytait.com.au**

Seb chairs – Jardan, **jardan.com.au**

Cushion
Bonnie & Neil, **bonnieandneil.com.au**

Primary artwork – Stephen Ormandy
Olsen Irwin, **olsenirwin.com**

P 188 – Blue Reef matt acrylic paint
Porter's Paints, **porterspaints.com**

Manta Dining Chair, cushion, ottoman, Missoni throw and large Balloons floor light – Spence and Lyda, **spenceandlyda.com.au**

Black Sisal rug
The Natural Floorcovering Centre, **naturalfloor.com.au**

Botanical Enquiry 03 framed photographic print
Daniel Shipp, **danielshipp.com**

Jamie Durie for Riva 1920
Ficus and Bungalow Stools
Jamie Durie, **jamiedurie.com**

Liquid Moon resin table and flower vase
Dinosaur Designs, **dinosaurdesigns.com.au**

Dark Floral wallpaper roll
Ellie Cashman Designs, **elliecashmandesign.com**

Leather KS Chair
Great Dane Furniture, **greatdanefurniture.com**

P 192–195 –
Floral cushions
Ellie Cashman Design, **elliecashmandesign.com**

Woollen felt blanket
Jacqueline Fink/Little Dandelion, **littledandelion.com**

Overland matt acrylic paint colour
Porter's Paints, **porterspaints.com**

Desert photograph
Ross Lawrence – MCM House, **mcmhouse.com**

Big Bug rotating armchair
Poliform, **poliform.com.au**

Indigenous timber painted bowl, Pop & Scott planter and ceramics on table
Koskela, **koskela.com.au**

Jamie Durie Gabion coffee and side tables
Jamie Durie, **jamiedurie.com**

LXVI chair C1780 with gold velvet fabric and silk velvet embroidered cushion, The Country Trader, **thecountrytrader.com.au**

Olive tree and other plants – Eden Garden Centre, **edengardens.com.au**

LLT207 Texas flooring
Karndean Looselay range,
karndean.com

White and graphite bedlinen
In The Sac, **inthesac.com.au**

Spillray pendant lights
Mondo Luce, **mondoluce.com**

Blue Magenta, 2015 – Alesandro Ljubicic, **alesandroljubicic.com**
scottliveseygalleries.com
michaelreid.com.au

Coral Tree on stand and concrete pig statues – Shades Of Pale, Hunters Hill
02 9817 4310

P 196–199
Zigrino wallpaper in Jet colour and Maidenhair matt acrylic paint
Porter's Paints, **porterspaints.com**

Table and chandelier
Shades Of Pale, Hunter's Hill
02 9817 4310

Cedar bath tub, basin and Vertical Greenwall Blanket
Jamie Durie, **jamiedurie.com**

Rattan chair and metal ice bucket
Oneworld Collections,
oneworldcollection.com.au

Plants – Eden Garden Centre,
edengardens.com.au

Concrete mushroom statue
Ici Et La, **icietla.com.au**

Green café chairs and green metal stand
Parterre Garden, **parterre.com.au**

Round bamboo frame mirror
Ginkgo Leaf, **ginkgoleaf.com.au**

Railway yard timber box on castors
Doug Up On Bourke,
douguponbourke.com.au

Bathroom towels, soap and toiletries and fur pelts – Koskela, **koskela.com.au**

Cosmic Hiro stool, towel stand, freestanding shelves, all in Coal and Hansgrohe Puravida chrome extended basin mixer and bath taps
Rogerseller, **rogerseller.com.au**

Fire Log wax candles
Top 3 By Design, **top3.com.au**

P 200–203
Walls painted in horizontal stripes from bottom to top: Dark Gully Green, Gully Green, Timberline, Olive Grove matt acrylic paint
Porter's Paints, **porterspaints.com**

AAP03 Black Oak parquet floor
Art Select Range Karndean Flooring,
karndean.com

Global round dining table, Kiki dining chairs, Vaughan console table and collection of terracotta vessels
MCM House, **mcmhouse.com**

Black sisal rug – The Natural Floorcovering Centre, **naturalfloor.com.au**

Black and white dinner plates
Koskela, **koskela.com.au**

Ostrich and flamingo framed prints
Imagine-This, **imagine-this.com.au**

Black sesame chiffon cake
Black Star Pastry, **blackstarpastry.com.au**

Black rubber plants – Eden Garden Centre, **edengardens.com.au**

P 204–207 – Linen and velvet drapes
No Chintz, **nochintz.com**
Motti sofa, blue & white porcelain planters, black and white painted log side tables/stools
MCM House, **mcmhouse.com**

Vintage Japanese and batik cushions, brass tray and cup and saucer
Planet, **planetfurniture.com.au**

Concrete leaf planter
Parterre Garden, **parterre.com.au**

Plants – Eden Garden Centre,
edengardens.com.au

Goccia decorative glass pendant light
Mondo Luce, **mondoluce.com**

Japanese zen garden/coffee table
Ginkgo Leaf, **ginkgoleaf.com.au**

Woollen felt woven wall hanging, basket & throw
Jacqueline Fink/Little Dandelion
littledandelion.com

Overcast matt acrylic paint on walls
Porter's Paints, **porterspaints.com**

P 208–211
Terra Verde rugs – Horizon Collection by Jamie Durie; Pony Rider circular rug
The Rug Collection,
therugcollection.com.au

Jamie Durie Brickwood coffee table, Float lounge and Bungalow stool for Riva 1920 – Jamie Durie,
jamiedurie.com

Rustic timber and metal trestle table
Doug Up On Bourke Street,
douguponbourke.com.au

Paintings
Ali Wood, **aliwoodart.com**

Harper armchair in blue and Sunday desk chairs in grey
Jardan, **jardan.com.au**

Hoodie integrated desk with woven Yuta Badayala hood and pendant light and Regina Wilson textile throw
Koskela, **koskela.com.au**

Zamia furfuracea in large terracotta pot and *Michelia alba* in cauldron bowl in bronze colour
Garden Life, **gardenlife.com.au**

Watermelon Margarita matt acrylic paint
Porter's Paints, **porterspaints.com**

Copenhagen console desk
Interior Classics, **interiorclassics.com.au**

Staccato bookshelf
Anibou, **anibou.com.au**

Vintage handkerchief planter with bromeliad and cherry sculptures
Selma Calheira, Brazil Parterre Garden, **parterre.com.au**

Begonia teal cushion
Bonnie and Neil,
bonnieandneil.com.au

Keshiki potted plant on desk
Ginkgo Leaf, **ginkgoleaf.com.au**

Large totem and small boulder beeswax candles
Dinosaur Designs,
dinosaurdesigns.com.au

P 214–217
Birch log four poster bed
Society Inc., **thesocietyinc.com.au**

Dark floral wallpaper
Ellie Cashman Design,
elliecashmandesign.com

Reindeer hide
Shades Of Pale, Hunters Hill NSW
02 9817 4310

Hemp knitted blanket
Jacqueline Fink/Little Dandelion,
littledandelion.com

White and cement bedlinen
In The Sac, **inthesac.com.au**

Classic bleached White Teak laminate floors
Quick-Step Flooring,
quick-step.com.au

Watermark matt acrylic paint
Porter's Paints, **porterspaints.com**

Bell copper side table Classicon
Anibou, **anibou.com.au**

Brass circular side table
Oneworld Collection,
oneworldcollection.com.au

Rustic timber and metal trestle table
Doug Up On Bourke Street,
douguponbourke.com.au

White leather daybed, pleated woollen throw rug and scatter cushions
Top 3 By Design, **top3.com.au**

Battery operated LED miniature Japanese paper lanterns
Gingko Leaf, **ginkgoleaf.com.au**

Tiny LED string of lights
Mama Papa, **mamapapa.com.au**

P 218–221
All kids' furniture (beds, bedside tables, table and stool set, desk and stool, upholstered ottoman, pendant light and coat rack)
Lilly & Lolly, **lillyandlolly.com.au**

Plants from Eden Garden Centre
Eden Garden Centre,
edengardens.com.au

Watermark and Evergreen matt acrylic
Porter's Paints, **porterspaints.com**

Neptune and Canary Zinnia rugs
Armadillo, **armadillo-co.com**

Kids budgie, pigeon and goldfish bedlinen – Top 3 By Design,
top3.com.au

Tee-pee, signature rosettes and patchwork quilts – Skinny Wolf,
skinnywolf.com.au

Black and white stripe painted branch
Silverblue, **silverblue.org.au**

Large dinosaurs
Terrific Scientific,
terrificscientific.com.au

Feather headdress and owl
Mama Papa, **mamapapa.com.au**

Colourful weaving – Natalie Miller
Koskela, **koskela.com.au**

Felt and fabric planters
Koskela, **koskela.com.au**

P 222–225
Walls painted in Watermark matt acrylic and Chalkboard paint in rust colour
Porter's Paints, **porterspaints.com**

Early kauri pine sideboard hutch base
Doug Up On Bourke Street,
douguponbourke.com.au

Dining setting: Bench, table, chairs and stool all part of Ilse Crawford's dining setting manufactured by De La Espada for Studioilse
Anibou, **anibou.com.au**

Jamie Durie plant integrated bench
Jamie Durie, **jamiedurie.com**

All cushions – Bonnie and Neil,
bonnieandneil.com.au

Yuta Badayala woven pendant lights – Koskela, **koskela.com.au**

White crockery and antique scales
The Bay Tree, **thebaytree.com.au**

Yellow crockery – Batch Ceramics,
batchceramics.com.au

Canterbury buffet
Freedom, **freedom.com.au**

Stenstorp kitchen island bench
Ikea, **ikea.com**

Natural varnished oak laminate flooring – Quick Step Flooring, **quick-step.com.au**

600x300x20 stone – Lavagrigia sawn (ignimbrite) on outdoor floors
Bisanna Tiles, **bisanna.com.au**

Plants – Eden Garden Centre, **edengardens.com.au**

Red artwork – Julie Paterson, **juliepaterson.com.au**

Ethnicraft oak shelving
Click On Furniture, **clickonfurniture.com.au**

Basket planter – Oneworld, **oneworldcollection.com.au**

Serengeti weave runner
Armadillo, **armadillo-co.com**

Copper colour painted fruit sculptures
Selma Calheira, Brazil
Parterre Garden, **parterre.com.au**

Resin flower bowl and platter
Dinosaur Designs, **dinosaurdesigns.com.au**

P 226–229
Inside: 600x300x20 stone – Lavagrigia sawn (ignimbrite); and outside: 600x600x15 stone – Gris San Vicente Flamed (limestone)
Bisanna, **bisanna.com.au**

Rock Salt and Watermark matt acrylic paint Porter's Paints, **porterspaints.com**

Grey sisal rug
The Natural Floorcovering Centre, **naturalfloor.com.au**

Primary artwork – Stephen Ormandy
Olsen Irwin, **olsenirwin.com**

Jil coffee table and Mini Softline planters in Oyster and Claypot from Tait, **madebytait.com.au**

Seb chairs in pastel blue with navy and mustard seat cushions
Jardan, **jardan.com.au**

Ida chair in Elephant Grey linen sling, Nomah armchair and Airlie side table – Eco Outdoor, **ecooutdoor.com.au**

Scatter cushions – Bonnie & Neil, **bonnieandneil.com.au**

Wall dot and printed ottoman
Pony Rider, **ponyrider.com.au**

Thinking swing
Pop & Scott, **popandscott.com**

Zinc tub – Ici Et La, **icietla.com.au**

Plants – Eden Garden Centre, **edengardens.com.au**

P 230–233 – Plants – Eden Garden Centre, **edengardens.com.au**
Panorama matt acrylic paint
Porter's Paints, **porterspaints.com**

Natural varnished oak laminate flooring – Quick Step Flooring, **quick-step.com.au**

600x600x15 stone – Gris San Vicente Flamed (limestone)
Bisanna, **bisanna.com.au**

Kartell Audrey black and white chair – Space Furniture, **spacefurniture.com.au**

Palm Print 1 & 2, *Eames House* print – Chris Turnham; *Hunter/Hunters* prints (sharks/kittens and dugongs/bunnies) – Kozyndan
Outre Gallery, **outregallery.com**

Antique painted French shutters, wire industrial basket pendant lamp, decorative porcelain roses and blue French enamel letters
Elements I Love, **elementsilove.com**

Jamie Durie Home Nelson setting – Jamie Durie, **jamiedurie.com,** covered in orange Poppy outdoor fabric and trestle table top from The Blume Collection Signature Prints, **signatureprints.com.au**

Shibori cowhide – Jacqueline Fink/Little Dandelion, **littledandelion.com**

Blue floral cushion – Bonnie and Neil, **bonnieandneil.com.au**

Large blue painted concrete pot with yucca plant
MCM House, **mcmhouse.com**

Lazy Season pot (on trestle table)
The Fortynine Studio and The Planthunter, **thefortynine.com.au, theplanthunter.com.au**

Large bonsai pot
The Gingko Leaf, **ginkgoleaf.com.au**

P 238–247 –
Artwork: *Earthwork 2* – William Delafield Cook
Olsen Irwin, **olsenirwin.com**

Bedlinen – In The Sac
inthesac.com.au

Crystals on dining table
phillippa.com.au

Pale pink ceramics
koskela, **koskela.com.au**

P 309 – Artwork Tracey Deep

Photography & design credits

Cover – House on a Dune:
Karen Fuchs © Karen Fuchs
Architect: Chad Oppenheim/Oppenheim Architecture – oppenoffice.com
Endpapers: Nick Bowers © Nick Bowers
P i: Nick Bowers © Nick Bowers
P i–iii: Laziz Hamani and Robert Reck © Oppenheim Architecture
Architect: Oppenheim Architecture – oppenoffice.com
P iv: Nick Bowers © Nick Bowers
P vi: Jamie Durie © JPD Media + Design
P 3–5: Nick Bowers © Nick Bowers
Styling: Corinna Koch
P 6: Vlad G Shutterstock.com © Vlad G
P 9: Jamie Durie © JPD Media + Design
P 10: Nick Bowers © Nick Bowers
P 13: Jamie Durie © JPD Media + Design
P 15: Nick Bowers © Nick Bowers
P 17: Alinta Lim © Durie Design
P 19: Riva 1920 © Riva1920
P 20–40: Tonya McCahon © JPD Media + Design
P 42–61: Nick Bowers © Nick Bowers
P 62: Laziz Hamani and Robert Reck © Laziz Hamani and Robert Reck
Architecture: Oppenheim Architecture – oppenoffice.com
P 63: Richard Powers © Power House
P 66: Richard Powers © Power House,
Architect: Yabu Pushelberg – yabupushelberg.com
P 68–9: Murray Fredericks © Nobbs Radford Architects
Architect/Interior Design/Landscape Design: Nobbs Radford Architects – nobbsradford.com.au
P 70–1: Richard Powers © Power House
Architect: Jacobsen Arquitetura – jacobsenarquitectura.com
P 72–3: Richard Powers © Power House
Architect: Bernardes Arquitetura – bernardesarq.com.br
P 74–5: Brett Boardman © Brett Boardman
Architect: Scale Architecture – scalearchitecture.com
P 76–7: Brent Darby © Brent Darby
Interior design: Alison Henry – alisonhenry.com
P 78–9: Daniel Shipp © Daniel Shipp
Interior design: Jane Stark/Stark Design – starkdesign.com.au
P 80–93: Richard Powers © Richard Powers
Architects: Jonathan Marvel & Shuji Suzumori – marvelarchitects.com, suzumori.org
Interior design: James Houston – mindspacedesign.com
P 94: Jamie Durie © JPD Media + Design
P 95: Jennifer Soo © Jennifer Soo/Sunday Life
P 95: Nick Bowers © Nick Bowers
P 96: Nick Bowers © Nick Bowers
P 98: © Hotel Im Wassertum
P 101: Jennifer Soo © Jennifer Soo/Sunday Life
P 103: Daniel Shipp © Daniel Shipp
P 104–19: Nick Bowers © Nick Bowers
Styling: Corinna Koch
P 120–1: Brent Darby © Brent Darby
Styling: Elke Brown
Interior Design & Furniture: Occa-Home – occa-home.co.uk
P 122–4: Nick Bowers © Nick Bowers
P 127: Simon Kenny © Simon Kenny
P 128–31: Nick Bowers © Nick Bowers
P 133: Greg Cox © Bureaux
P 134–7: Nick Bowers © Nick Bowers
P 139: Richard Gooding © Richard Gooding
Interior design:
Staffan Tollgård Design Group – tollgard.co.uk
P 140–3: Nick Bowers © Nick Bowers
P 144–5: Light Locations © Light Locations
P 146: Nick Bowers © Nick Bowers
Styling: Corinna Koch
P 147: Jamie Durie © JPD Media + Design
P 148: Daniel Shipp © Daniel Shipp
P 150–1: Jennifer Soo © Jennifer Soo/Sunday Life
Interior design: Hecker Guthrie – heckerguthrie.com
P 152: red table/pumpkins © Edward Addeo
P 152: butterfly pendants © Daniel Shipp
P 153: interiors © Nick Bowers
P 153: diffuser © Jennifer Soo/Sunday Life
P 154–5: Shinoki/AMKK © Shinoki/AMKK
Artwork: Azuma Makoto – azumamakoto.com
P 156–7: Nick Bowers © Nick Bowers
P 158: Armelle Habib © Armelle Habib/*Sunday Life*
Stylist: Heather Nette King
P 159: Tonya McCahon © JPD Media + Design
P 160–1: Jennifer Soo © Jennifer Soo/*Sunday Life*
P 162–4: JPD Media + Design © JPD Media + Design
P 166–7: Jennifer Soo © Jennifer Soo/*Sunday Life*
P 168: Jennifer Soo © Jennifer Soo/*Sunday Life*
P 170–1: bathroom © Jennifer Soo/*Sunday Life;* living room © Armelle Habib/Sunday Life
Stylist: Heather Nette King
P 172: Armelle Habib © Armelle Habib/Sunday Life
Stylist: Heather Nette King
P 174: Nick Bowers © Nick Bowers
P 175–9: Jennifer Soo © Jennifer Soo/*Sunday Life*
P 180: Nick Bowers © Nick Bowers
P 181: Jardine Hansen © Jardine Botanic
P 182: Laziz Hamani and Robert Reck © Oppenheim Architecture – oppenoffice.com
P 183: Nicholas Watt © Nicholas Watt
P 184: Tonya McCahon © JPD Media & Design
P 185: Tonya McCahon © JPD Media & Design
P 186–233: Nick Bowers © Nick Bowers
P 234–5: P 251: Matthew Bannister © DBOX 2014
Architect: Chad Oppenheim/Oppenheim Architecture – oppenoffice.com
P 236: Marie Claire Bordaz © Marie Claire/Bordaz
Architect: XY Architecture
P 238–247: Nick Bowers © Nick Bowers
P 248–249: Karen Fusch © Karen Fusch
Architect: Chad Oppenheim/Oppenheim Architecture – oppenoffice.com
P 251: Matthew Bannister © DBOX 2014
Architect: Chad Oppenheim/Oppenheim Architecture – oppenoffice.com
P 252–9: Yuta Yamada/Fujishokai
Architects: Sumiou Mizumoto/Yoshitaka Kuga ALTS Design Office – alts-design.com
P 260–7: Yuta Yamada/Fujishokai
Architects: Sumiou Mizumoto/Yoshitaka Kuga ALTS Design Office – alts-design.com
P 268–77: Laziz Hamani and Robert Reck © Laziz Hamani and Robert Reck
Architecture: Oppenheim Architecture – oppenoffice.com
P 278–83: Marie Claire Bordaz © Marie Claire/Bordaz
Architect: XY Architecture – xyarchitecture.com
P 284–93: Shannon McGrath © Shannon McGrath/Studiofour
Architect: Studiofour – studiofournews.com
P 294–7: Paul Massey © Paul Massey
Chef: Skye Gyngell
Interior Design: Briony Fitzgerald Design
P 298–305: Edward Addeo © Edward Addeo
Interior Design: Dransfield & Ross
P 306: Nick Bowers © Nick Bowers
P 309: Nicholas Watt © Nicholas Watt
P 314: Edward Addeo © Edward Addeo

Index

A
air, using the element of 153
Ananda Lake House, The Catskills 80–93
animal motifs 152
art 183

B
B&B Italia 138
Barda, Walter 44, 50
bathrooms 196–199
baths 34, 50, 89
Batterson, Virgine 111
Bawa, Geoffrey 155, 308
bedrooms 192–195, 214–217, 218–221
Birchgrove House, Sydney 68–69
bonsai 174
bowl of cherries (design inspiration) 134–139
bringing the outdoors in 146–185
- art 183
- flowers 180
- found objects 178
- lighting 184
- outdoor furniture 185
- plants 161–177
- sunlight and shade 159
- *wabi sabi* 182

Bungalow collection 16, 18–19
Bush, Nadine 54, 189, 307, 309
BV House, Brazil 70–71

C
candles 156
Chelsea Townhouse 76–77
cherries (design inspiration) 134–139
Cherryfields, New Jersey 298–305
Citterio, Antonio 138
colour 14–15
- as design concept 102
- palettes 15

cooling 59–60
Cooper, Mark 126

D
decorative lighting 189
design concepts 100–103
- layers of design 103

design DNA 7–8
design inspiration 99
designed space 105
- examples of 106–145

dining rooms 200–203, 222–225
Durie, Jamie 307–308
- Jamie's homes 20–39, 42–57

E
edible gardens 39
egg (design inspiration) 105–115
elkhorns 170, 173
entertaining areas 50
environmental aspects 59–60

F
Ficus stool 16–17
fire, indoors 156
flowers
- bringing the outdoors in 180
- design inspiration 140–145
- floral motifs 152
- frozen in ice 155

foliage (design inspiration) 122–127
form, in design 100
found objects 178
functional lighting 189
furniture
- design of 2, 16–19, 103, 111
- outdoor furniture indoors 185

G
gardens 39 *see also* indoor plants
- interior 156
- vertical 39, 50, 59

Guarujá Beach House 72–73

H
hanging plants 166, 169
heating 59–60
House on a Dune, The Bahamas 248–259
house plants *see* indoor plants
Houston, James 80–93

I
imperfection, the art of (*wabi sabi*) 182
indoor plants 161–177 *see also* plants
- favourites 162–164
- hanging plants 166, 169
- health of 165
- interior gardens 156
- miniature gardens 174–175

indoor-outdoor spaces *see* transterior living
industrial space, room 'sets' in 186–233
inside-out zones *see* transterior living
inspiration sources 94–145 *see also* natural elements
interior design style 11 *see also* bringing the outdoors in; transterior living
- room 'sets' 186–233

interior gardens *see* indoor plants
interiors 5–60

J
Jamie's home, Los Angeles 20–39
- garden 39
- home 26–34
- studio 22, 27

Jamie's home, Sydney 42–57
- home 50, 54
- outdoors 54

Japanese architecture 27, 34, 50

K
Kaspar, Marcella 126
kids' bedrooms 218–221
kitchen/dining 54, 222–225
Kofunaki House, Japan 260–267

L
La Muna, Aspen, Colorado 268–277
layers of design 103
lighting 27, 50
- bringing the outdoors in 184
- functional and decorative 189
- sunlight and shade 159

line, in design 100
living rooms 204–207
lofts 208–211
Long Courtyard House, Sydney 74–75
'luxescaping' 64

M
Maison JMD, Paris 278–283
Makoto, Azuma 155
Marvel, Jonathan 84
Maxalto Eunice dining chairs 138
miniature gardens, indoor 174–175
Modern-Shed 22
mood boards 108, 118, 124, 130, 136, 142
Mosman House, Sydney 78–79
Moss Residence, Sydney 238–247
motifs from nature 152
movement, in design 102

N
natural elements 1–2 *see also* designed space
bringing the outdoors in 149–157
- getting the look 41
- inspiration sources 96
- natural materials 151
- sustainable features 59–60
- using 153

Navone, Paola 111
New York Design Depot 2
Newson, Marc 7

O
objets d'art 178
Occa-Home Urban Look 120
organic materials *see* natural elements
outdoor furniture indoors 185
outdoor rooms 39, 54, 308 *see also* bringing the outdoors in

P
pebble, rock, stone, twig (design inspiration) 128–133
plants 27, 34, 50, 54, 59–60 *see also* indoor plants
- bringing the outdoors in 161–177

Platycerium spp. 170, 173
Porter's paint 188
pot plants *see* bonsai; indoor plants
proportion, in design 102

R
rhythm, in design 102
Ridge Road Residence, Melbourne 284–293
rock gardens, indoors 156
room 'sets' 186–233

S
salt & pepper (design inspiration) 116–121
scale, in design 102
Scandi influences 120
shade and sunlight 159
shape, in design 100
solar energy 59–60
space, in design 100
spatial awareness 12
split-level areas 50, 192–195, 214–217
Spring Restaurant, London 294–297
Sri Lanka 155, 308
Staffan Tollgård Design Group 138
staghorns 170, 173
stockist lists 311–312
sunlight and shade 159, 184
sunrooms 226–229
sustainable features 59–60
Suzumori, Shuji 84
swimming pools 54

T
terrariums 175–177
textiles 2
texture, in design 102
timber 7
- baths 34

transterior living
- case studies 236–307
- defined 64–65
- design philosophy 63–93
- inside-out zones 213
- Jamie's homes 22, 44

V
vertical gardens 39, 50, 59

W
wabi sabi (art of imperfection) 182
warehouse space, room 'sets' in 186–233
water features 155
water use 59
wood 7, 34
workrooms 230–233
Wright, Frank Lloyd 12, 27
- sunlight and shade 159

Z
zen gardens, indoors 156

LANTERN

UK | USA | Canada | Ireland
Australia | India | New Zealand
South Africa | China

Penguin Books is part of the
Penguin Random House group
of companies whose addresses
can be found at global.penguinrandomhouse.com.

Penguin Random House Australia

First published by Penguin Random House Australia Pty Ltd, 2016.

10 9 8 7 6 5 4 3 2 1

Design by Evi O. © Penguin Random House Australia Pty Ltd
Typeset in Futura by Evi O.
Colour separation by Splitting Image Colour Studio, Clayton, Victoria
Printed and bound in China by RR Donnelley Asia Printing Solutions Ltd

National Library of Australia
Cataloguing-in-Publication data:

Durie, Jamie, author.
Living design / Jamie Durie, Nadine Bush.
9781921383090 (hardback)
Includes index.
Interior decoration.
Bush, Nadine, author.

729.24

penguin.com.au/lantern